'A tarot reading guide for people who aren't wholly sure that they are witchy enough to be into tarot. It's just the right balance of cosmic mystery and straight-talking sense.'

Caroline O'Donoghue, author of *All Our Hidden Gifts* and *Promising Young Women*

'I absolutely ADORED *Wild Card*, which I DEVOURED – it is precisely the sane, wise, welcoming, inclusive, beautiful and sensitive introduction to the cards I needed when I was learning, and it really is going straight to the top of my recommended tarot books. I loved it in every particular, and will be pressing it on every tarot learner I can find.'

Alice Tarbuck, author of *A Spell in the Wild*

'An indispensable guide to the tarot for both the seasoned reader and the novice. Up there with *78 Degrees of Wisdom*, but with its own brand of no-nonsense expertise and guidance, as well as being beautifully illustrated, it's a classic for a new generation and a fun, friendly companion on anyone's tarot journey. I loved it.'

Rhiannon Lucy Cosslett, author of *The Tyranny of Lost Things*

'A deeply humane exploration of tarot awash with cultural references, humour and stories. A thoroughly modern (and welcome) reinvigoration of the tarot handbook.'

Sinéad Gleeson, author of *Constellations*

'A beautiful, playful, intriguing book.'

Nina Stibbe, author of *Love, Nina* and *Reasons to be Cheerful*

Wild Card

JEN COWNIE AND FIONA LENSVELT

WILD CARD

Let the Tarot Tell
Your Story

bluebird
books for life

First published 2022 by Bluebird

This paperback edition first published 2023 by Bluebird
an imprint of Pan Macmillan
The Smithson, 6 Briset Street, London EC1M 5NR
EU representative: Macmillan Publishers Ireland Ltd, 1st Floor,
The Liffey Trust Centre, 117–126 Sheriff Street Upper,
Dublin 1, D01 YC43
Associated companies throughout the world
www.panmacmillan.com

ISBN 978-1-5290-8211-1

5 7 9 8 6 4

A CIP catalogue record for this book is available from the British Library.

Illustrations by Mel Four

Typeset in MillerText by Jouve (UK), Milton Keynes
Printed and bound by CPI Group (UK) Ltd, Croydon, CR0 4YY

Visit **www.panmacmillan.com/bluebird** to read more about all our books
and to buy them. You will also find features, author interviews and
news of any author events, and you can sign up for e-newsletters
so that you're always first to hear about our new releases.

Contents

The Lovers

I was always afraid
of the next card

the psychic would turn
over for us-

       Forgive me
for not knowing
how we were

every card in the deck.

Timothy Liu,
from *Don't Go Back To Sleep*
(Saturnalia Books, 2014)

CHAPTER 1

Hello, Friend . . .

What do you feel when you think of tarot cards? If you're frightened, don't be. If you're curious, that's more like it. These cards are not what they seem. In fact, they're probably not what you've been told at all – they don't really prophecise doom or promise glory. But they are magic in their own small way. Each one has a story to tell: turn a card over and it can transport you to the past, illuminate the present, or ask questions of the future. It can help you to listen to the whispers of your subconscious mind, or hold up a lens through which to look again, closer this time, at the experiences that have made you who you are. Every card in the tarot is a wildcard, a portal to the unexpected. Every time you draw your cards, you open up possibilities. What will appear and what will you see in them? What lessons could they offer up? What aspects of yourself might they reveal?

The tarot is a very old practice. The earliest surviving decks of cards date from the mid-fifteenth century, and it's probable that the earliest decks ever made and used are older still. It was originally a game (in some cultures, it still is) and in its standard form, its structure isn't so different from that of common or garden playing cards. It has four suits that run Ace to Ten with courts of Kings, Queens, and their retinues; plus an additional twenty-two trump cards – the famous ones which you have likely heard of, even if you've never picked up a tarot deck before. But what really makes the tarot special is that over the last six hundred or so years that it has existed, each of those seventy-eight cards has become imbued with meaning and symbolic significance. Each one is full to the brim with secrets and stories and questions.

Spread the cards out before you and you'll find mythical images that draw you into a world of kings and queens, hanged men and magicians, sparkling skies, crowns made of moons, chained devils, and women who tame lions. These cards are wild not just in the sense that they offer up surprises and invite in the unexpected, but in the sense that they remain untamed. The tarot is a growing and changing thing. There are myriad decks with different designs, and as many subtle shades of interpretation for each of the cards as there are readers. These cards are an encyclopaedia of experience and emotion: archetypes and narratives that anyone and everyone might encounter and explore – whether that's by accepting them, challenging them, or finding a new lens through which to understand them.

In *Storming the Gates of Paradise*, Rebecca Solnit writes, 'The stars we are given. The constellations we make. That is to say, stars exist in the cosmos, but constellations are the imaginary lines we draw between them, the readings we give the sky, the stories we tell.' You can think of the tarot in the same way: there is an established set of basic meanings for the standard tarot deck, but what makes this practice so rewarding is the pattern dance of the cards, the associations they prompt for different people, and the unique connections they forge in each individual mind.

The tarot as we know it today was codified in the early twentieth century by a group known as The Hermetic Order of The Golden Dawn (quite the name, isn't it?). This collective, which counted the poet W. B. Yeats among its members, is also the originator of the most well-known tarot deck, the Rider Waite Smith tarot (RWS). This is the basis for almost all modern decks. Sometimes you'll see it referred to only as the Rider Waite deck, after its publisher, Rider Company, and academic author, Arthur Waite, but we much prefer the name which recognises the extremely significant – some might even say, fundamental – contribution of its artist, Pamela Colman Smith. The imagery and meanings of that deck are often the starting point of tarot reading, but they are by no means everything. We'll not only introduce you to the common iconography and interpretations of the RWS, but also help you to navigate the tarot on your own terms, with whichever version of the deck you choose to read from.

What we won't do is speak to you about psychic practice, for the simple reason that it isn't something we know about and it's not how we use the cards. Reading the tarot without being a clairvoyant doesn't make it any less powerful. For us, the magic of the cards lies not in fortune-telling, but in storytelling. Tarot readings have given us, and those we read for, new perspectives through which to approach aspects of our lives and selves. They can help make sense of places, feelings, and actions in an often chaotic world. Sometimes they offer up the chance to open up about subjects that might not otherwise be discussed, in ways that you might not otherwise discuss them. The cards don't provide yes-and-no answers, but they can offer understanding, prompt conversations, guide people to new paths, and, sometimes, just hold space to acknowledge the more difficult feelings and moments in life.

The tarot has long been associated with various mystic, religious and occult practices, from astrology to Wicca – but it's not a package deal. You do not, by taking up one, automatically subscribe to them all. When we were training as tarot readers, our tutor also gave us an introduction to spellwork, inviting us to perform rituals as part of a group. It was fascinating, a little eerie... and definitely not for either of us. We don't know anything useful about crystals, cannot guess your star sign, and have never journeyed on the astral plane (though we will both admit to an unusual level of interest in the moon). Tarot practice intersects with many different disciplines, skill sets, and belief systems. Those overlaps can be valuable and enriching, but they aren't obligatory – and if you wish to engage with those practices, it's best to first seek out instruction from an appropriate teacher. But the truth is, the cards don't belong to a single community, and there isn't only one way to use them. Anyone can read the tarot, and everyone should feel welcome to do so.

For us, the most powerful connection isn't between the cards and witchcraft; it's between the oral story-telling tradition and tarot: fairy tale and folklore, myth and legend. For millennia, humans all over the world have tried to make sense of their fate by tapping into time-worn narratives and stories that are far bigger than just one life. The written word was the preserve of the elite for a very long time, and even the concept of authorship has only existed for a relatively small portion of human history. Stories used to be allowed to run wild, passing from one teller to the next, and adapting to new environments and changing circumstances. Even those that might seem to have a fixed form – books of fairy tales as recorded by Charles Perrault or the Brothers Grimm, or the classical myths as recounted by Ovid or Homer – are really only an impression of the story as told in one moment, by one person, within one culture. Those tales also exist in myriad other versions and other tellings, both ancient and modern, springing from different minds, communities and context – and are no less important or meaningful for not having been taught in schools. The most enduring stories, the ones we all know, cannot be owned or tamed. They have always found ways to put out tendrils of fresh growth, and take on new shapes as the world around them changes.

The tarot is exactly the same as those ancient, yet evergreen, tales. It is formed of archetypes and familiar narratives that have been traced and retraced over hundreds of years and by thousands of voices, becoming ever richer and more beautiful as they develop new layers of meaning. There is no single way to read the cards – no such thing as right or wrong – only a collective understanding of their symbolism to which each and every one of us is invited to add our own nuances and our own interpretations.

In the introduction to her collection of fairy tales, Angela Carter wrote that those stories represent 'the extraordinary richness and diversity of responses to the same common predicament – being alive.' She could just as well have been writing about the tarot: a deck of cards that somehow holds within it all the strange, wonderful, sad, and lovely things of life – and in which there is always space to find more. The tarot can help you to place what you are going through in a broader context; it can help you to feel less alone; and it can help you to access wisdom and advice that has remained valuable and true throughout centuries of human experience.

When we read for other people, we tell them that there is no card that won't, in some way, feel familiar. You are in every card in the deck, and every card of the deck is within you. The tarot offers you a chance to step back from your life and see it not as a series of disconnected moments and experiences, but as a story writ large. And it can be empowering to do so: when you see your life as a narrative, with arcs and patterns and repeated characters, you realise that you might actually have more control over it than you'd realised. You can't always decide what happens to you, let alone predict it, but you can certainly think about how you want to respond to it, and how you want it to shape your sense of self. As Joan Didion wrote in *The White Album*, 'We tell ourselves stories in order to live.'

At its heart, the tarot is a storytelling device, a way of framing a question or an experience through symbols and archetypes. These are all familiar stories, and the tarot helps reveal the lessons and the collective knowledge contained within each one. It is timeless, ageless, and it is fluid. In this book, we hope to offer up a starting point, and show you how these cards might apply to you and your journey, no matter how different or difficult your story has been. We'll talk you through the commonly held meanings of each of the cards, explain their significance and the questions they most often ask of a reader, and share some of the more personal associations and stories that they bring up for us – just as we might if we were sitting in front of you with a deck of cards. And, just as we would in that scenario, we invite you to consider your own interpretations of each card as you go along.

Pulling cards and exploring the patterns between them is a way to open up a conversation. It's an opportunity for self-reflection and self-knowledge and, perhaps, a way to make sense of your own story. Don't be afraid to listen to what comes up for you as you get to know the cards, and as you begin to see them in the potentially millions of different combinations and permutations in which they can fall when you're reading them in sequence. Make notes on what the patterns remind you of, and what else you see in them. That's the very essence of what it means to read the tarot.

Finally, you'll notice that there are two of us here. Sometimes you'll hear one voice saying 'I', sometimes another, and sometimes, as now, we'll speak together. There will be points at which you'll be able to work out whose story you're reading, and plenty where you won't. Given what we've just told you about the essential nature of the tarot – its multiplicity, its complexity, the fact that it comes out of a tradition of many voices speaking in chorus, echoing through the centuries – we hope you'll forgive us that quirk. And we hope that, in time, you'll want to add your own voice, and your own ways of telling these tales, to ours.

CHAPTER 2

Secrets of the Tarot

One of the things that we love about the tarot is that it's full of surprises. No matter how long you practise it, there's always more to learn, more stories to discover, and more ways to interpret the cards. It's a game with no end, a conversation that never gets stale. It's a practice that can't easily be pigeonholed – it resists definition, and different people use it in different ways. This is wonderful... but it does make it hard to learn how to use the cards, what their limits might be, and what an ethical practice of the tarot might look like.

So, before we introduce you to the cards themselves, we wanted to share the answers to the questions we're most commonly asked about the tarot – and the questions that we wish someone had answered for us when we first started out.

1. Can I predict the future with the tarot?

This is the question that we get asked most often. And the (un) helpful answer is that, to a certain extent, it's a decision that you get to make for yourself – Jen always tells querents* that

---

* In case you were wondering, 'querent' is the technical, and fancy, term for the subject of a tarot reading – the person for whom you are reading the cards. It means 'the one who seeks'.

she won't give predictions; Fiona is more open to it, depending on the situation. What we both agree on is that reading futures with the tarot isn't fortune-telling in the traditional sense: this is not about getting a sneak preview of what's to come. Instead, reading the future through the tarot is more psychological than supernatural.

As the psychoanalyst Carl Jung said: 'We can predict the future when we know how the present moment evolved from the past.' Quite often, whether it's in our personal lives, our work, or in science fiction, we gaze into the crystal ball and expend all our energy on trying to predict what will be changed and different and unrecognisable in the future. We forget that the future is always a product of the past and that, although some things change, plenty stays the same. There are enduring truths, needs, experiences, and trajectories – frankly, if there weren't, nobody would find a centuries-old divination tool useful.

In other words, reading the tarot to predict what will happen actually means extrapolating on what's going on now. If someone is behaving in a certain way, or taking a particular approach, then literally thousands of years' worth of similar stories can give you a fairly accurate idea of what might happen next – or what they might do to change course. Broken down and stripped of its fortune-teller connotations, a good tarot reading is a way of re-examining the present, narrating the past, and discussing the future. The tarot reader isn't in control, nor is the deck: the querent is.

2. Will the tarot tell me what to do?

It would be wonderful, not to mention convenient, if a deck of cards could reveal hidden truths, locate future partners, perhaps do a little light communication with the dead, and furnish you with next week's winning lottery numbers. When you're dodging the arrows of fortune, whether that's matters of the heart or the general anxiety of what you should be doing with your life, there could be nothing more reassuring than a sign from the universe that your path is the right one. It would be nice to have confirmation that whatever struggle you're facing – whether that's going on your hundredth sub-par date, deciding whether to change jobs, or figuring out why things don't seem to happen for you in the way they happen for others – has some greater purpose. (Because, dear god, it had better.)

Sadly, the tarot doesn't deal in straight answers. In fact, mostly it answers questions with questions. Sometimes it even answers questions with riddles (thanks, tarot). But it also doesn't *not* give you solutions. What we mean by that is that the tarot is not a passive exercise; it's an active one. It shows you ways that you might think about things differently. It might offer up a suggestion for how to approach a problem. It might help you to reflect on what you've been doing that isn't working for you. It might ask you to confront something that's been troubling you, but that you've been sticking your head in the sand about. It might say something deeply inconvenient to hear. Or it might help you feel more confident in following your instincts.

If you're expecting detailed instructions on what to do with your life, you're going to be disappointed. The cards are symbols, not signposts – and, let's be honest, you've almost certainly got enough people, publications, and unseen forces trying to influence your decisions. But if you're looking for new perspectives, and prompts that will help you reflect on your actions, beliefs, and behaviours, you've come to the right pack of cards.

3. Can I peer into someone else's life with them?

Read for yourself, read for others, read for pairs of people about their relationship with one another if you like. Pull a card to help you understand your feelings about another person, even if you've not seen them in years – or pull ten cards to help you pick apart your feelings about ten other people. The key thing here is: *your* feelings.

Reading tarot cards for somebody who isn't there to have a conversation with you is a bit odd and, to be honest, unlikely to offer you much in the way of useful insight. It won't tell you anything about their perspective; it'd just be an exercise in projection, which is never a healthy thing to do.

In short, there isn't exactly a printed tarot code of ethics, but if there were, it would say: no, you should not do that.

4. Aren't tarot readers just watching people's facial expressions and then responding to them?

The answer to this is 'not no', and there's a very good reason why. A lot of the complaints you'll hear about the tarot – or indeed any type of divination or psychic work – focus on the idea that their practitioners are people who are just really good at analysing their clients' body language and responses to questions and statements. The truth is they probably are good at it.

But I'd argue that there's another way of looking at it. The tarot can be a way of offering something that most people don't actually experience often in day-to-day life: active and supportive listening. If I'm reading your tarot, then you can rest assured that I am listening very carefully to anything you say, and I'm tuned into your tone, inflection, and all of your subtle non-verbal cues because I should be. A tarot reading is not about the tarot reader. It's not a chance to showboat or prove how clever and magical you are. It's an opportunity to open up a dialogue: sometimes between a reader and a querent, and sometimes just between the querent and themself.

And if, as a reader, you're not listening and watching carefully to see how your querent is feeling and what might be coming up for them, and if you're not responding with kindness and care and empathy, then I'm afraid you're doing it wrong. Nobody needs to be told that their new relationship is destined to fail because a card says so: it's not helpful, and it's not true. Nor do they need to be sold a future to make them feel better. You should talk to your querent about what a card means and ask them what comes up for them – particularly if it's a difficult card – not because you need to prove that the tarot works, but because they deserve to have an experience that's helpful rather than depressing and disempowering. Never be ashamed of listening closely.

5. What do I actually need to know to read the tarot?

There are three things you really need to know about in order to dabble in the tarot with confidence. Firstly, you need to have a working knowledge of what the cards mean. This is, without question, the hardest part of learning to read the tarot. But if you really want to enjoy reading, you just have to take the plunge and start committing those core meanings to memory – doing so is the difference between reading a newspaper in a foreign language, and reading a newspaper in a foreign language by painstakingly looking up every single world in a dictionary. Fortunately for us all, the tarot is, famously, an illustrated deck of cards, so you've always got a picture to jog your memory with each one.

Secondly, you need to be able to see how the context of a reading influences which of a card's many subtle shades of meaning is coming to the fore. Once you've got a good sense of the cards' basic symbolism, you can start to play with spreads of multiple cards. Spreads are patterns in which each position represents something: for example, a card to symbolise your current situation, and a card to symbolise a challenge you face. This is where the depth and complexity of tarot symbolism really comes into its own: you get to look at each one and explore its meaning through the lens of its position in the pattern. Your job is literally to read: to look at the way the cards have fallen, and see what kind of story it tells. This is an art, rather than a science – an art that relies on intuition and creativity.

Finally, you need to imagine how the cards interact with one another. Odd as this might sound, you need to think about your tarot cards as having relationships with one another, and explore what those relationships are when you see them in a spread. Some cards belong to the same family; others are sworn enemies. Some share a very similar vibe, expressed at different volumes; others are stark contrasts. Cards can have multiplier effects, or cancel one another out. As you begin to become more familiar with the deck, those relationships will gradually come into sharper focus.

6. Are there cards I should be afraid of?

I once gave a three-card reading to an acquaintance of mine whose gloomy outlook on life was basically a personal brand. 'I'm probably going to get all of the terrible cards,' she said, with characteristic pessimism, before pulling Death, The Tower, and the Ten of Swords, which are, by most people's standards, The Terrible Cards. But she's absolutely fine – in fact, she thought it was hilarious. The moral of this story, and the short answer to the question, is that, while some of the cards have grimmer reputations or speak to difficult truths, not one of them can hurt you.

The longer answer lies in the origins of the cards. The thing to remember about the tarot is that it's been around since at least the fifteenth century. And the thing about the fifteenth century in Europe is that it was, by all accounts, quite different to the modern-day world. Religion was a very big deal for everyone, for example, and death felt rather more immediate. Swords and other melee weapons were considered acceptable elements of daytime attire for some parts of the population. All of which is to say – the basic visual symbolism of the tarot is rooted in quite different cultural norms to our own, and should not always be judged by our own modern standards.

There are some cards that look pretty alarming: the Grim Reaper riding a horse over a field of the dead; a man lying face down with ten (yes, ten) swords in his back; a portrait of Satan. What is true of all of these images is that they are, and always have been, visual metaphors – it's just that they're not familiar ones for people who live in a world of mobile phones and air travel and medical science. (This is one reason why so many artists and designers reinterpret the tarot through a modern lens.) Some cards might seem better or worse on the surface but, in reality, every single one has the capacity to speak to both good times and difficult times. I can't promise that they won't sometimes prompt reflection on hurts, fears, and traumas. But what I can say with absolute certainty is that not a single one of them is a warning of terrible things to come, and none of them should be feared.

7. What do I do if a card is upside down in a reading?

Some people read reverses – in which the orientation of the card determines whether you read a card's positive or negative aspects – and some people don't. Neither of us reads reverses because it feels too prescriptive and too limiting. Every card offers both gifts and challenges, a light side and a shadow side, and you should always consider both elements of its meaning when finding your interpretation.

Sometimes it's extremely obvious which way the card is leaning. At other times, the position of the card in the spread and the context of the reading should be enough to help you decide which meaning has the upper hand. For example, if you came across the Ace of Cups in a spread, which speaks to emotional and creative potential, there are two broad sides to the reading. One is positive: it's about having a huge amount to offer and being ready to put yourself out in the world. The other is a little more pessimistic: it speaks to times when you might be pouring your heart into a relationship or a project which isn't going anywhere, and might even be damaging or exhausting you.

A tarot practitioner who reads reverses would only consider that second set of meanings if the Ace of Cups appeared upside down in a spread, whereas we would advise you to make your interpretation based on the context. If the Ace is appearing for your querent as a card of challenge, for example, that's the time when it's most likely to be useful to delve into its shadow meaning – not when you've just shuffled in such a way that it comes out upside down.

Occasionally, you won't have an immediate sense of which side of the card is dominant today – and there are some cards that seem to flip between their two sides more easily than others. When that happens, the best thing to do is remain open. Feel out the different angles and see what resonates. The tarot is a bit like a Rorschach test: if you're seeing something in the inkblot, it's probably because it's something that, subconsciously, you know you need to express. In the same way, if a querent reacts strongly to one aspect of a card, it probably means it's brought up something that they need to pay attention to.

8. Is being a tarot reader like being a therapist?

As you explore the cards, you'll notice that the stories in the tarot confront some of the most challenging and fraught aspects of being alive. Conversations around mental health aren't uncommon. This is one of the tarot's greatest consolations: readings create space for these emotions. The ritual of reading, of actively listening to yourself, or truly connecting with another, is a valuable one. It can feel therapeutic; it can be a way of practising mindfulness and grounding yourself; and, for some people, it's a good way of checking in with their mental health. But no, tarot readers are not therapists, nor should they be seen as a replacement for professional care. (And I say this as someone who both reads the tarot and has a long-term therapist, and has discussed the relationship between the two.)

On a practical level, this does have some implications for how you use the cards. If you are reading for other people, especially if those people are strangers, there is a scenario for which you should be prepared. Tarot readings can bring up a lot of difficult emotions. Sometimes a person might ask you for a reading knowing full well that they're processing something difficult and hoping that the tarot might help them to make sense of it.

And sometimes a person might come for a reading for a bit of fun, and surprise themselves with the depth and intensity of feelings that it provokes in them. If you read for other people, you will at some point or another experience someone – a friend, a colleague, a stranger – bursting into tears. This can be quite unnerving. And it's likely to be even more unnerving for the person doing the crying, which is why the best thing you can possibly do when it happens is to be a human being who is witnessing another human being's sadness. Ask them if they're alright, if they need a hug, or a cup of tea, or if there's anything they need to talk about. Be a friend, even if you don't know them, and even if only for ten minutes. You might never know (or might only find out years later) how much of a difference your kindness made.

9. How do I know if I'm doing it right?

There's one sure-fire way to know if you're doing tarot right, and that's whether or not it's a useful or enjoyable experience for you and for the person whose cards you're reading – which is possibly also you. If someone is hating every second of the experience, then maybe it's time to re-evaluate the approach. But if it's fun, or interesting, or thought-provoking, then it doesn't matter whether you're a seasoned tarot reader with years of experience, or a rookie dabbler with a rudimentary understanding of the cards. If it's working for you, then it's working.

And when it's not working, it's usually pretty obvious. My first professional reading was one such occasion. The tarot reader sat me down and, with little preamble, began, 'This has been an especially trying time for you and I'm afraid that it isn't going to get easier.' She went on, at length, unstoppable even when I told her there wasn't a great deal of drama in my life at the time. I just felt a little directionless. I was in my twenties and everything in life felt precarious, because it was. Was she confusing my past with my present? She was unrelenting: no, I was about to encounter the lowest point in my life and should be prepared for trouble ahead. Lovely. Also, as it turned out, completely incorrect.

The person who read for me that day was trying to tell me a story about my life, and place me at the centre of it – it's just that she went about it the wrong way and ended up disempowering me. That experience was one of the many that shaped how I began to use the tarot: not as a magic trick, but as a navigation tool – a map that shows the routes taken by people born long before us, and where those paths led them. I practise with the principle that just because you see it in a tarot reading, doesn't mean you have to say it. Ask questions, rather than making assumptions. It's far better to lean into the subjectivity. Let the cards act as prompts rather than prescriptions and worry less about being 'right' and more about allowing enough space for the full story to unfold.

10. I have more questions!

Don't we all! We're about to dive into the structure of the deck and, most importantly, the meanings of each of the cards. But never fear – at the end of the book, we'll return to some more practical guidance on learning and reading the tarot, as well as a list of resources to help you advance your practice.

CHAPTER 3

Suits You

Welcome to the Minor Arcana. Don't be fooled by the word 'minor'. The four suits of the Minor Arcana make up the majority of the tarot deck – and within these fifty-six cards is all of life.

If you're just starting out with the tarot, you might feel like the right thing to do is to jump straight into the Majors: they're the most recognisable cards, after all, and their names generally feel quite straightforward. But looks can be deceiving. The twenty-two Majors are heavy with meaning, each owning multiple layers of symbolism and metaphor: they are the wildest cards of the deck. We strongly recommend getting to know the smaller creatures of the Minor Arcana first.

That's not to say that they can't also be a little daunting. There are a lot of Minor cards and their naming conventions don't, at first glance, give you much of a clue as to their meanings. Even fully illustrated, as they are in most tarot decks, they generally aren't what you'd describe as self-explanatory. If you came across the Two of Pentacles, for example – a card traditionally represented by a person in a very large and jazzy hat, doing a juggling dance on the beach – you would be well within your rights to wonder what on earth is happening. And the Minors are almost all that way: a lot of pictures of small figures enthusiastically going about their very obscure business. But once you get your eye in, the miniature tableaux on each of the cards do, mostly, begin to make sense. (Only mostly, though.)

The good news about the Minor Arcana is that it is broadly governed by patterns, in a sort of grid system. Each card has a suit – like a playing card deck, only more dramatic – and a number or court position. Each card's meaning is closely tied to its suit and its number position so, once you've learnt the pattern for one suit, you'll find the other three much quicker to get your head around. The less good news is that there are always exceptions to the rules, and subtleties of interpretation. But deciphering those intricacies is half the fun of the tarot. To get you started, here are the basic patterns of the Minor Arcana.

Cups, Wands, Swords, Pentacles

The four suits of the tarot are sometimes renamed in different deck designs – an artist might choose to represent a suit as moths or a type of flower if that fits with their creative concept. But they're most commonly referred to in the Rider Waite Smith tradition of Cups, Wands, Swords, and Pentacles and, no matter what deck you're reading from, you should quite easily be able to work out the correspondence of suits.

Each of the suits is aligned with an element: Cups are water, Wands are fire, the Swords are air, and Pentacles are earth. In almost every deck, the iconography of the cards links back to those elemental divisions. Knowing the element of each suit helps you to understand it: the suit's element is the basis of its metaphors, the raw materials from which its stories are built. The four suits and four elements represent different aspects of life, with each element corresponding to a different part of the self, and a different type of action. When you begin to use card spreads, pay attention if you see a preponderance of one particular suit, which might point to that part of your querent's life being foregrounded in the reading.

There's a more detailed introduction to each suit in their card chapters, but it's worth having the big-picture overview before you learn about each of them individually:

The **Cups** are the suit of the heart. If they have a verb, it is 'feeling'. They're an encyclopaedia of emotion, linked to all kinds of relationships, and to creativity and inspiration.

The **Pentacles** are the earthy suit of the body, of things that are real and manifest. They speak to health, wealth, home and hearth. They are about being and making: the things you have, and the things you lack.

The **Swords** speak to the mind. They represent thoughts: invisible and intangible like their element, air, but nevertheless extraordinarily powerful. The verb of this suit is 'thinking' (and, some would say, also its good friend 'overthinking').

The **Wands** are about energy in its rawest sense – the soul, or the spirit. They are all about doing: where you channel your willpower; how and if you are able to fuel your inner flame and bring it to bear in your life.

Painting by Numbers

Next, there are the cards' positions in each suit. If you're familiar with normal playing cards (and to be honest, even if you aren't), this should be a fairly easy concept to grasp. There are fourteen cards in each suit, numbered ace to ten, followed by the court cards. Unlike a standard playing card deck, there are four of these: Page, Knight, Queen, and King. Across the four suits, the cards which share the same position all have a similar role to play and story to tell – so, if you know one, you can often extrapolate its sister cards.

There are three important things to know before you learn the significance of each of the positions.

The first is that in each suit, the numbered cards tell a story that you can follow through from beginning to end. The story isn't a traditional one, and probably wouldn't make for a very good novel, but it's straightforward: it's about starting out with the possibility of something, and then gradually getting more and more of it. In other words, the energy of each suit builds and builds until you end up with a whole lot of it. In many decks, particularly the Rider Waite Smith, you'll see this depicted quite literally on the cards: whatever the element of the suit is, you see more and more of it in the illustrations as you work your way through the suit. So, in the Pentacles, you start out with an empty landscape, and by the end, you see a busy, bustling city. The position of a card in its suit can be read as an indicator of how far through a journey the querent is, which can be useful in a reading.

The second thing to know is that, while the structure of the journeys in the number cards is the same, the outcomes go one of two ways. The Cups and the Pentacles share a similar destination; the Swords and the Wands have quite another. And those outcomes are linked to the nature of the suit. The rule of thumb is this: you can never have too many Cups or Pentacles, but fewer Swords and Wands is generally better. If it's round, then go for your life, try to catch them all, etc. If it's pointy... approach with caution.

The third and final thing to know is that the court cards (Page, Knight, Queen, King) are weird. They're weird enough that, later on, we've given them their own chapter with more details on how to read them. But, broadly speaking, these anthropomorphic cards represent aspects of yourself, or people in your life.

So, without further ado, the Minor Arcana positions, one by one:

The **Aces** are the source of each suit, representing the opportunities and potential of its energy. They are raw and as yet unfocused: they ask you to consider what you have to offer, and what you want.

The **Twos** are the most simple, uncomplicated expression of the suit's energy. They are its bread and butter, the daily tasks of the suit. They ask if that energy is balanced and flowing, or if it's blocked.

The **Threes** are experiences that embody the power of the suit. They tend to speak to things you need to do to strengthen yourself and grow, and to how you interact with others.

The **Fours** are a chance to catch your breath on the journey. They're a little pause – safe spaces, stable and restful, if sometimes a little stale. They ask you to take stock of where you are, and how you're doing.

The **Fives** are places of discomfort within the suit. They're challenges, conflicts, and difficulties faced. They don't usually ask you to do anything – instead they ask you to sit with the feeling.

The **Sixes** are shifts in balances of power and moments of transition. They often deal with the interplay between times past, present, and future. They ask what you've learned so far, and what you'll do with that knowledge.

The **Sevens** are moments of evaluation and decision-making. They ask you to really interrogate your actions, beliefs, and feelings. They speak to honesty – and sometimes to the lack thereof.

The **Eights** are the point at which you find the transformative power of the suit and channel it to bring about change. They aren't always easy moments, but they're satisfying.

The **Nines** are entirely focused on what it means to be an individual who has built up a lot of that suit's energy. This, as you will see, can be a good place to be, or a very, very worrying one. They offer a glimpse of what's to come at the end of the journey.

The **Tens** represent completion, the end of the cycle. They are the ultimate outcome of the suit's energy, for better or worse. And they ask you what you'll do next.

The **Pages** are youthful, naive, almost childlike characters. They embody the energy of the suit in its embryonic stages, where everything seems possible, you don't make assumptions based on prior experience, and rules don't really exist.

The **Knights** are doers. They are characters who have taken the energy of their suit to its logical extreme – i.e. probably too far. They have turned the volume of the suit up to the maximum. It's a lot.

The **Queens** are characters who have achieved a balanced, sophisticated, and yet intuitive understanding of the suit. They bring it to bear in their own lives, and hold space for others to do so too.

The **Kings** are characters who have true mastery of the suit. They harness its energy and bring it to heel. They can be forces for good, and beacons in the darkness. They can also be awful.

As you may already be able to imagine, the interplay of suit and card position speaks to an extraordinarily broad spectrum of emotions, experiences, and perspectives within the Minor Arcana. The patterns give structure and shape to the deck but, as you begin to get to know the cards, you'll see how it's the subtleties that really matter. The greatest stories aren't just the broad brush strokes of narrative arcs: they live in the tiniest details, the minutiae of life.

CHAPTER 4

The Cups

The suit of the Cups deals with the element of water, which should, even on a visual level, give you a sense of how these cards behave. Water has range, and it's not biddable. It can find its way through the tiniest cracks, it can move mountains (or, at least, persist for aeons in slowly grinding them into dust), and you absolutely cannot push it up a hill. Water is mutable, a shapeshifter, it goes where it goes, whether you like it or not.

In the world of the tarot, therefore, water means feelings. Emotions, like water, can run deep, can change in a moment, can overwhelm you or wear you down. All you can really do is try to manage them – try to find a way to hold them that makes them a little more understandable and gives them a little bit of shape. And that, of course, is where cups come in. They are a vessel for containing feelings (even if only temporarily). In short, they deal with matters of the heart.

When we say 'heart', you might automatically leap to 'love'. And you wouldn't be wrong, but you wouldn't be entirely right, either. Love is here in all its many guises: the Cups speak of romance, friendship, family. But love is far from the only thing that calls the heart its home. Creativity lives in the Cups: this is the suit of the subconscious, of dreams, and of inspiration. It also has a fruity side: fantasies, passion, pleasure, indulgence, hedonism, hunger, and satiety. And the Cups offer, as is only appropriate for the element of water, moments of reflection. Intuition belongs in this suit, as does grief, healing, closure, and fulfilment.

When Cups appear in a reading, particularly if they do so in abundance – or to the exclusion of all else – it generally leads to emotional conversations. If you're reading someone's tarot, you're hopefully already asking your querent how they're feeling, but the Cups can offer some more specific signposts on whereabouts, within the wide, wild territories of the human heart, you ought to focus your attention today. Sometimes, you'll meet people who say they always pull Cups, or you might find that they often appear when you're reading for yourself. You can set as much or as little store by that as you like, but it's fair to say there are some people who just have Cups energy: people who live with their hearts on their sleeves, who are guided by their emotions, rushing, capricious, often impossible to contain.

And sometimes the opposite is true. Sometimes, the Cups point to what's lacking. They can lead to conversations about caged hearts and stifled creativity. Not everyone is able to give their feelings free range. Not everyone has been taught, or encouraged, to do so without fear of retribution. For those who might not feel comfortable with candid expressions of emotion, or who might struggle to articulate their feelings directly, this suit can prompt difficult conversations. For those people these cards, handled with care, can be some of the most powerful facilitators of communication in the tarot.

The Cups are usually nourishing cards. They're gentler than the other suits, and certainly possessed of rather more subtlety and tact than the Majors – particularly when it comes to the way they're depicted in most decks (only one person looks miserable, and no one is dead!). But there's more to them than tranquil surfaces. These cards aren't shallow: hidden currents abound, and there are treasures, shipwrecks, and fantastical beasts to be found in their depths. As we like to say, and as is surely not at all unnerving to hear: 'Come on in! The water is ... changeable.'

ACE OF CUPS

ABUNDANCE, POTENTIAL, CREATIVE ABILITY, OPENNESS, LOVE,
GENEROSITY, VULNERABILITY, MISPLACED FEELINGS

If there is one thing that the internet has told us many times, it is that there is a strong case for cats being a liquid. The evidence: they can fit themselves perfectly into any shape of vessel available to them, flush against all surfaces, no corner left unfilled. There is apparently no space into which a cat cannot pour itself, and then exhibit great contentment with itself for having done so.

This is the image to hold in your mind when the Ace of Cups turns up in a tarot reading. When this card appears, a metaphorical liquid cat is at large. Someone has the opportunity to decide what shape and volume of space they would like to take up in the world. And frankly, they have a lot of options! The world is their oyster, their shoebox, their pan, their sink, their novelty vase, their hiking sock – whatever. This card signals an abundance of possibilities. It is usually depicted as one very large cup which literally runneth over, as though the cup has no bottom, as though it is somehow a wellspring which will never dry up. It speaks to someone who is brimming with potential – this being the Cups, usually creative potential, or emotional potential – but hasn't yet decided where to channel it.

In many ways, and in most appearances, then, this is a lovely card. It says that a querent has a lot to give the world, that their reservoirs are deep, untapped, possibly even bottomless. It invites you to ask where they want to direct their creativity, their feelings, their loves. Is it time to embark on a new project? Are they ready to invite a new relationship into their lives? (Maybe a partner, maybe something else – a friend, a pet, a houseplant.) It asks what their heart wants, and where it will go; what it will make, and what it will make of them. It says that they have enough paint to fill a canvas – or a thousand canvases – and that they have enough love to sustain something new and vital. It is, for the most part, a hopeful card, a card that looks to the future with bright eyes.

But do be conscious of where this card falls in a spread, and do listen if this optimism doesn't seem to chime with a person – or if it feels like something they once had, but have lost. Some people have an abundance of potential, and find it drained away from them by trying to do too much at once, like a bucket pricked with a hundred tiny holes. Others have an endless supply of love to give, but channel it into the wrong place or the wrong person: a hungry, empty void that can never be sated, and for which they can never be enough.

There are times when having a bottomless heart can be a dangerous thing. It can take a while to realise that you should never have to drain yourself for anyone or anything. But if you find a vessel that feels like a good fit for you, one that looks like it'll be able to hold you in a shape that you'll find pleasing while you bask in the sunshine, the Ace of Cups invites you to hop in and fill it up.

QUESTIONS TO ASK WHEN YOU SEE THIS CARD: Where do you want to channel your potential? Do you feel ready to start something new? What does your heart want or need? Are you putting yourself into the right things? Do you have more to give?

TWO OF CUPS

UNION, CONNECTION, MARRIAGE, PARTNERSHIPS, HEALTHY
RELATIONSHIPS, CREATIVE FLOW, BALANCE, ME TIME

Querents always want The Lovers to appear in their tarot readings when they're in love. Of course they do. The Lovers is the stuff of epic romances, power ballads, and daydreams. Who wouldn't want that for themselves? But if you ask a tarot reader what card they would want to see in a reading about relationships, they would probably choose the Two of Cups instead. This isn't a card about spiritual connection or ideals or fantasies. This is a card that is grounded in the physical and worldly aspects of a relationship: it asks, does this actually work? And how?

When we see Twos in the tarot, they ask whether the suit's energy is blocked or flowing, and here that energy is emotional. This is a card about connection. And not just any old common garden sort of connection: the sort that has reciprocity, and no power struggles, and mutual understanding. It's the sort where the partners think about the other's needs as well as their own, where there's a balance between what's given and what's taken. It's the card of secure attachment styles and open communication. How VERY healthy. When the Two of Cups appears, it's an opportunity to give your relationship an MOT: what is working? Are there areas that might require improvement? Do you feel you can be open with your partner? If particular subjects cause friction, why might that be?

While the Two of Cups isn't always about *love* love, it also... isn't not. Often, people do want to talk about romantic relationships when they see this card. In the Rider Waite Smith deck, the Two of Cups depicts a couple coming together in a ritual that looks a lot like a wedding. For some people, that is what it might literally represent: am I getting married?; am I about to get engaged?; do I want to get engaged?; why is everyone getting engaged?; how do I feel about marriage?; I'm going to a wedding! But it is worth pointing out that this isn't solely a card for lovers: it's a card that encompasses all sorts of equitable relationships and attachments, from a friendship, to the relationship between a faithful human and their faithful hound, to a business partnership, and any other combination you can imagine. So for you, this card might represent how connected you feel to those around you.

This card can also speak to the relationship you have with yourself (if you don't have love and compassion for yourself, who will you have it for?). It can characterise that sense of creative flow when everything comes together, when all the parts of yourself are integrated and working in harmony; when you are making magic happen. Not all of the greatest duos are romantic duos. So when you see the Two of Cups, think of the joy of connections in the broadest of senses. And ask yourself, how are yours faring? Are they balanced? What do you need from them? What are you giving them?

QUESTIONS TO ASK WHEN YOU SEE THIS CARD: Which relationships in your life give you energy and vice versa? What place have romantic relationships had in your life? What do you expect from a current relationship? Do you feel understood? Are you expressing yourself in the most healthy way? How do you feel in your own company, and how do you feel in the company of others?

THREE OF CUPS

FRIENDSHIP, RELATIONSHIPS IN A BROAD SENSE, COLLABORATION,
GOOD TIMES AND CELEBRATION, DISLOCATION

The Three of Cups – which is depicted in the Rider Waite Smith by three women dancing around, wearing cracking frocks, and holding chalices in the air – is about one thing, and one thing only: the joy and power of friendship. And it's a particular kind of friendship: the kind where there's no such thing as personal space, no such thing as too much information. It's a place where you can be yourself, and be vulnerable.

This card is a reminder that friendships ought to be celebrated. They ought to be tended like a garden. Whether you have rolling grounds, an allotment, or a humble window box, it doesn't matter: the point is that whenever you find a connection, treasure it and help it to grow. Friends are there before lovers are – and sometimes they're around for much longer. They can be the family and the community that you create for yourself, particularly when relationships with biological families are strained. But we don't have the same set of terms to describe those relationships – best friend? Work wife? Like a sister? My ride or die? A window box? These are blunt, euphemistic tools. Maybe part of the problem is that the rules of friendships aren't those of a romantic or of a familial relationship. You don't owe each other the same things; you have to make up your mind how you want to play it and your road isn't as clearly marked.

And it's still too easy for friendships – particularly female friendships – to be written off as a holding pattern for people who haven't yet achieved society's great dream: successfully identifying and settling down with The One. This is, obviously, nonsense. Friendships aren't a consolation prize. They are vital. They shape and teach us who we are and can be. They show us the edges of ourselves and round off our sharp bits (or sharpen them further, if needs be).

When Jen and I became single at the same time in our mid-twenties, we had many conversations that revolved around the question of whether we were actually any good at being in relationships. The conclusion we drew was that while we would rather leave some encounters off our romantic CVs, one thing was never in doubt: that, in our friendship, we had built something wonderful a different kind of relationship, but no less important for being so. Our love for each other has endured time and distance. We've faced challenges separately and together, and overcome them. We care for one another, practically and emotionally. We've learnt about arguing badly and disagreeing healthily. We dote upon one another. As needed, we're one another's plus one for parties, weddings, and adventures. Our friendship is basically an ever-fixed mark that has looked on tempests and never been (permanently) shaken – really, it's the stuff of epic poetry, Hallmark movies, and shared jokes that mean nothing to anyone else. It's a Three of Cups friendship.

When you see this card, it's a reminder of the value of friendships and connections. And it can be a reminder of the dislocation you can feel when you're not in step with those around you. When friendships aren't thriving, when you're at a transition point in life, when you move somewhere new or feel like you're surrounded by people with whom you have absolutely nothing in common, you can quickly come untethered. But it only takes one friend, one person to relate to, one familiar face at a coffee shop counter, to begin turning that around. So invest in people. Cherish them. Cheers to them.

QUESTIONS TO ASK WHEN YOU SEE THIS CARD: **What connections do you value most? How have those friendships shaped you? Which connections take energy from you? What kind of a friend are you?**

FOUR OF CUPS

OPPORTUNITIES, DECISIONS, EXPECTATIONS, OBLIGATIONS,
EVALUATION, DISSATISFACTION, EXCITEMENT

In the tarot, the appearance of a Cups card rarely causes alarm.
Cups are arguably the nicest of the suits, the friendliest: they're
about feelings, love, and creativity. Most people want more of
this in their lives. You can never have too many cups! Or can
you? The Four of Cups is here to talk to you about exactly that.

Every time you see a Four in the tarot, it's offering you
breathing space; a rest on your journey. Sit down. Consider
your trajectory – where are you going? Is it the right way?
The Four of Cups is a literal depiction of that moment. In the
Rider Waite Smith, we see a person with three very nice cups

to their name, sitting around, minding their own business. Behind them, a mysterious force offers up a fourth. The cup itself can represent any number of things: an emotional connection, a creative opportunity, a new feeling, whether painful or delightful, or even just an offer of assistance. In and of itself, the cup is neither good nor bad, right nor wrong. It doesn't presuppose a correct answer, but it poses a question, and a decision to be made: do you want it? Do you want this thing – whatever it is – that's being offered to you?

The gift of this card is choice: you can accept the thing, or you can say no to it, and both options are totally valid. The challenge often lies in separating what you want and need from what might be expected of you; the external forces that might sway your hand one way or the other. When this card appears in a reading, it's important to note what it brings up; what your gut tells you it refers to. And then it's important to sit and try, if you can, to identify your preconceptions and biases. Ask yourself, what is the *should* in this situation? What decision do I feel like I'm supposed to make? What do other people – society, culture, my family, my peers – expect me to say? And is that the same as what I *want* to do?

We all exist within structures. There are things we're told we're supposed to want, and things we are told we're not allowed to. Often enough, the should or shouldn't isn't about the thing itself, but about who we are and where we fit into society. I once read an extraordinary essay by Jess Zimmerman about hunger: specifically, about how the permissibility of hunger differs between the genders. 'A man's appetite can be hearty,' she writes, 'but a woman with an appetite is always voracious: her hunger always overreaches because it is not supposed to exist.' Sometimes, we are supposed to politely decline the fourth cup, to pretend not to want it, because we have plenty of cups already (thank you so much!). Other times, the cup feels like it's forced on us: of course you want to take on this new project or connection. It'd be rude not to.

The truth is it's not rude to say no, and it's not overreaching to say yes. Just be honest with yourself: do you want this?

QUESTIONS TO ASK WHEN YOU SEE THIS CARD: What opportunities are being offered to you right now? Do you feel under any obligations to accept or decline something? What do you really want to do, deep down? Are you hungry for something more? Do you need to give yourself permission to say no?

FIVE OF CUPS

LOSS, GRIEF, REGRET, PESSIMISM,
MOVING ON, ACCEPTANCE, HEALING

The Five of Cups delivers some intense emotions – in many decks, it's one of the cards that looks most ominous when it appears in a reading. And while it's a melancholy card that asks you to tread carefully with the feelings of your querent (even if that querent is you), it's also one of the cards that offers the greatest potential for catharsis.

In most decks, it features a forlorn figure who is turned away from the viewer, into the landscape of the card. In front of them, several cups have fallen over or shattered. These cups represent losses, disappointments, and failures: things that the card's character is focusing on to the exclusion of all else. The mood, to quote the old Nintendo quit screen message, is 'Everything not saved will be lost'. A person who is in the midst of a Five of Cups moment is not having a good time. They are sad, they are grieving, and, in all likelihood, they have good reason. This card is an acknowledgement of that feeling.

But usually, somewhere else in the card, there are more cups. These cups are upright and unbroken. They symbolise hope and opportunity – the things that aren't spilled, and aren't lost, even if you aren't able to see it just yet, even if you're still too preoccupied with what is gone. It's rare (though, of course, not beyond the bounds of possibility) that life deals a full strike of bad luck. And it's rarer still that there's no way out: no lantern, however small, left burning in the darkness to show you the way back.

The Five of Cups has two messages, knotted together, and worth picking at and picking apart. It's a reminder that loss is a part of life, and that grief is healthy. Sometimes when it appears, it's a sign that, while you might be obsessing about the cause of your pain, you haven't actually allowed yourself to properly feel the depths of it. The Five of Cups is a reminder that the only way forward is through: you can't hold back the tide when it comes to grief, or deny the truth of your losses. You can only do the work that's needed to integrate them into who you are, and who you'll become. And you can only do that once you've looked the beast in the eye, and called it by its true name.

This card is also a reminder that there comes a time when you need to be able to move on from your grief. It can appear when you cannot or will not allow yourself to look to the future – but when you must do exactly that. You cannot stop time, and nor should you want to. Sometimes, the Five nudges you to the realisation that the key to letting go is to lift your gaze so that you can see things that are still here, as well as those that you've lost.

In the RWS, the background of this card is a bridge that needs to be crossed: the path to the other side of your feelings. This card asks you, simply, what do you need to do to get there?

QUESTIONS TO ASK WHEN YOU SEE THIS CARD: Have you lost something or someone recently? Is there something you're missing or grieving? How are you feeling? Can you see anything to hope for or look forward to? Have you given yourself the time you need to feel your pain? Are you ready to move forward?

SIX OF CUPS

Phew! We went through a slightly rocky patch there with the Five. But don't worry. Grab yourself another cup, this is a chance to regroup.

The Six of Cups is one of the sweeter cards in the suit. If you were to give this card a name, it would be nostalgia. In most decks, particularly those based on the Rider Waite Smith, its depiction is like a faded family photo; a hazy dreamscape spilling over with flowers and barely recognisable figures. It's a little confusing and doesn't entirely make sense, as is often the case with childhood memories. You kind of have to go with it.

In its most literal reading, it invites you to get in touch with a past self. That might mean going back to old haunts or childhood homes, making contact with people you haven't seen in a while, or remembering people who are no longer with you. This won't be comfortable territory for everyone, particularly if your childhood or your past were difficult, or if your child self is not representative of who you are now. But what this card invites you to make space for is a moment of peace, happiness, connection, or contentment – whenever and whatever that was. Small moments like these can be profound: they give you a chance to consider what you are grateful for or what you are ready to leave behind.

Don't underplay the value that reflecting on the past might offer. Nostalgia can give people a sense of identity, it can make us feel as though we have roots, and it can make life seem more meaningful. On cold days, it has been observed that we can use nostalgia to literally feel warmer. Psychologist Dr Erica Hepper theorised in an interview with the *New York Times* that nostalgia can even help people to deal with transitions in life.

The tarot often symbolises change, and it doesn't shy away from the fact that change isn't always easy. How nice, then, that in the Six of Cups, we're offered some metaphorical bubble wrap against the bumps and bruises of our journey's endless unpredictability. In the constant dance of novelty-seeking and risk aversion that characterises human behaviour, this card is all about the joy of sticking to, or revisiting, known paths, and looking backwards rather than forwards. It's called a comfort bubble for a reason and there are times when it's exactly the right thing to do to sit in yours with a cup of tea, a Wagon Wheel, and some Saturday night television.

The other side of the Six of Cups is less about what you need, and more about what you can offer: your legacy. Our minds are always recreating the past, and as we get older, this intensifies. Philippa Perry writes in *How To Stay Sane* that 'it is our short-term memory that fades rather than our long-term memory. Perhaps we have evolved like this so that we are able to tell the younger generation about the stories and experiences that have formed us which may be important to subsequent generations if they are to thrive.' The Six of Cups asks what those stories might be for you.

QUESTIONS TO ASK WHEN YOU SEE THIS CARD: What stories do you tell about yourself when you meet people? What has the past gifted you? Where and when do you feel safe and comfortable? Is there anything you've lost as you've grown up that you'd like to regain? What will your legacy be?

SEVEN OF CUPS

DESIRE, DREAMS, FANTASY, IMAGINATION, AMBITION,
CHOICES, GREED, ILLUSION

One of the things to enjoy (or at least get your head around) about the tarot is that it loves drama. *Loves* it. Why say something in plain, unadorned language when you could ADD VIPERS???

This is the way of the Seven of Cups, the card of idle daydreams, fantasies, and deepest desires, be they honourable and noble or ambitious or spicy. This card tells you to pay attention to your emotions and reminds you to question what's going on behind the choices you make. The Rider Waite Smith depicts this with the image of a person gazing up at a row of seven cups, which float on a conveyor-belt of clouds. The chalices are overflowing with jewels and riches, temptations and mysteries, curses and skulls, dragons and... yes! Vipers! It's like a chaotic psychometric game-show and, indeed, sometimes we all feel exactly like that.

At its heart, this card is simply saying: you have feelings, and they are many and various. Some of them are healthy or benign; others not so much. This is your invitation to observe them, especially if you seem to be in thrall to them. It's a prompt to work out if what you see and believe about yourself and the world is grounded in reality or if it's an illusion. It asks you to dig beneath the surface of your fears and desires and ascertain their origins.

The Sevens in the tarot are all about doing something for yourself – and this card can, accordingly, symbolise new opportunities to act on your dreams and fantasies. It's a card that is pregnant with possibility, a smorgasbord of options laid out in front of you from which to select the most delectable morsels. But, as the strange objects depicted in the cups suggest, it's also a warning to not always take things at face value – particularly when it comes to the callings of the heart, or the workings of the imagination. Like the dishes served at a fairy feast, sometimes things that are delicious and tempting to the eye can turn to ashes and dirt in your mouth. These cups aren't real yet. Are you sure that they're an accurate representation of what's possible? Are you sure that you're being honest with yourself, and not conjuring an illusion or an idealised version of what you hope for? Is there a shadow in the dream that you're studiously refusing to acknowledge?

The Seven of Cups is telling you it's time to move towards action but to make sure that the feelings and intentions behind your decision are good. Because it's all very well imagining filling your mantelpiece with glorious chalices that everyone will admire – but have you told anybody yet about the vipers?

The novelist Kurt Vonnegut wrote in *Mother Night*, 'We are what we pretend to be so we must be careful about what we pretend to be.' This is a Seven of Cups sentiment. At the end of the day, you become what you repeatedly do. Sometimes it's only years later that you see the effects of your actions, so choose them consciously and choose them wisely.

QUESTIONS TO ASK WHEN YOU SEE THIS CARD: What goes through your mind when you daydream? Are there any patterns to your idle thoughts? Do you find yourself returning to the same concerns or anxieties or arguments? What would you do if you weren't afraid?

EIGHT OF CUPS

CLOSURE, MOVING ON, LEARNING, LOSS, NEW CHAPTERS,
NEW ADVENTURES

There is a saying that both Fiona and I have often used in reference to parties, but which neither of us is particularly good at adhering to: 'Leave while you're still having fun.' It's common knowledge that being the last person standing at any event is not even slightly cool. And yet, sometimes the night calls, your enthusiasm and natural *joie de vivre* answers... and the next thing you know, everyone else has gone home, and you're left with the knowledge that you would have much preferred to be one of those people (So elegant! So self-aware!) who noticed the turning of the tide and bowed out at precisely the right moment.

As it is with social events, so it is with many other things in life: they have a natural end point, a best-before date that should be observed, and often isn't. Because sometimes it's hard to stop, hard to let go. Sometimes it's even hard to see that you've overstayed your welcome until long after the dust has settled. There are very few people in the world who have not clung on to something a little too long: a once-lovely relationship that has soured; friendships that are no longer the right shape for the people in them; a dream that used to mean everything to you, but which doesn't seem to hold the same sparkle any more.

Change is inevitable, and often uncomfortable. The tarot often likes to remind its readers of that fact, and this card is one of its more direct statements on the matter. The Eight of Cups is the quieter and slightly less blunt sister of the Death card. It says that sometimes things end, whether you want them to or not, and that there's really no point in pretending otherwise. Not all relationships last, not all ideas come to fruition, not all homes (real or metaphorical) are forever. And it reminds you that, sometimes, when you try to hold on to those things for too long, you ruin what they were to you.

There is value in knowing when to call it a day, when to walk away from something that has run its course, when to make a graceful exit. It isn't always easy, but it can be an extraordinarily powerful action: it's freeing, certainly, but it's also an act of kindness and care, towards yourself and towards others. It allows you to preserve the memory of what you had and to look back on it with fondness – indeed, the Eight of Cups usually depicts someone walking away from eight cups, all of them upright and unbroken on the shoreline. It's a way of leaving peacefully, rather than with wreckage in your wake. Gwyneth

Paltrow might have popularised the phrase 'conscious uncoupling', but the tarot had the philosophy down long beforehand.

The gentle but firm message of the Eight of Cups is that it's alright to let go. It can appear when someone has just found closure, or when they need to. There are times when a scorched-earth policy might be for the best (see: The Tower), but when this card is around, you know it probably isn't one of them.

QUESTIONS TO ASK WHEN YOU SEE THIS CARD: Is there something in your life that's run its course and which you're still clinging on to? Is it time for you to let it go? Will fighting for it really give you the outcome you want? Have you recently let something go? Do you feel guilty about walking away? What would Gwyneth do?

NINE OF CUPS

PERSONAL SATISFACTION, ACHIEVEMENT, CONTENTMENT,
PLEASURE, INDULGENCE, DECADENCE, PRIDE

My goodness, what a lot of cups you have! Cups, cups, cups, as far as the eye can see. Rarely have I seen such an extravagant and varied array of vessels – and so beautifully displayed! I love this for you, I really do.

I like to describe this card as 'A Woman In Her Prime'. It should firstly be noted that anyone of any gender can be A Woman In Her Prime – this is the tarot and everything is metaphorical (the very jolly fellow on the Rider Waite Smith card definitely fits the bill, for a start). Indeed, I now have a number of male colleagues who have adopted this phrase and happily use it in day-to-day working life. They were introduced to it after I made it one of my New Year's resolutions: forget specific, measurable objectives; the goal for that year was to become someone who lives for her own pleasure and indulges in it without apology; who surrounds herself only with people she loves, and has an absolutely marvellous time. In short, someone of whom others might say, 'Ah, yes, there goes a woman in her prime.' Was the resolution achieved? Of course not. Do I regret making it? No, not at all.

The Nine of Cups is a card that asks you to take a moment to appreciate what's around you; the life that you have built for yourself; the friendships you've made; the things you've created. Sometimes, I think, we can be a little wary of putting all of our successes and joys out there, and saying, 'Behold the glory!' We can feel superstitious – do I really deserve this? Will these things be taken away from me if I seem to be proud of them? Is everything actually as good as it seems, or will I find disaster waiting for me around the next corner? Can I afford to stop? The Nine of Cups says that you do deserve this: what's more, this is something you made for yourself. These cups didn't just fall into your lap by chance. You forged them, and you are right to be pleased with them. You are right to pause and enjoy them.

This card is about living in the moment and truly experiencing the satisfactions – big or small – that doing so can offer you. It encourages indulgence: not putting off for the future what you can revel in right now. It tells you to throw caution to the wind and just live; immerse yourself in the things you love, and love the people you choose with all of your heart. Be a little bit silly if the mood takes you. Be romantic, be impulsive, be spontaneous. Enjoy the delights of the mind and the body.

Admire every single one of your well-turned cups, and invite other people to look at them too.

The shadow in the card is the knowledge that, yes, this pleasure is ephemeral. There will always be bad days ahead. There will always be new challenges to rise to, new goals to set yourself, new heights to scale. There's no such thing as a happy ending (more on this shortly in the Ten of Cups). But there is *here* and there is *now*, and sometimes, when it is bursting with sweetness, the only thing to do is to take a long, deep draught of it.

QUESTIONS TO ASK WHEN YOU SEE THIS CARD: What brings you satisfaction? What have you created for yourself that ought to be appreciated? How can you celebrate the good in the here and now? How do you define success? What makes you feel fulfilled? Are they the same thing? Are you denying feelings of pride? Are you worried about whether you are deserving? How can you indulge yourself today?

TEN OF CUPS

FAMILY, HAPPINESS, COMPLETION, JOY, UNMET
EXPECTATIONS, SELF-DOUBT

Well isn't this lovely? The Ten of Cups is often illustrated with a
family embracing and playing under an arch of gleaming cups
in a sunny sky. It's hard to think of a jollier scene in the Minor
Arcana. I know, I know, you've come to the tarot imagining
doom and portent at every corner and we're serving you rain-
bows. It's not what any of us expected. And to be honest, when
it crops up in readings, it often raises eyebrows. Is this how I
feel? Or how I'm meant to feel? Is this what happiness looks
like? Is this... good?

The first thing to say about the arrival of the Ten of Cups in a reading is that unlike, say, the Death card, this card largely does what it says on the tin. It represents joy, happiness, fulfilment, and family. If you're in a good place emotionally, it can signal a moment to stop and celebrate where you've got to in life. You have experienced emotional growth and you have found, at the end, contentment. This is not a bad place to be!

Yet what strikes a lot of people when they see the Ten of Cups in a reading is that maybe they're not quite there yet. Or maybe, for them, fulfilment doesn't look like the heteronormative family scene on the card. This card looks suspiciously like a Happily Ever After ending in a fairy tale, when the reality of life is far more nuanced and complex and untidy even at the best of times. Chasing the Ten of Cups can feel like chasing the rainbow: it is always moving just out of reach.

One of the big questions this card raises is, who am I meant to be? Today it feels like we're all faced with countless ideas about how we should live our lives. They're not always helpful and often they are conflicting. Be professionally successful! Find your passion! Also buy a home! Be beautiful but, for you! Be self-fulfilled! Live that single life! Also find love! Don't forget to have a baby! These social narratives of grow up, get a job, meet a partner, start a family offer time-worn paths that you can choose to follow. But ultimately, they're just stories, some of them very old, and some of them will, and others will not, suit you. It can be exhausting having to decide what you're supposed to do with yourself, and especially so when other people are choosing different paths that make you feel even more unsure about your own.

Jen and I prefer interpretations of the Ten of Cups that leave open the meaning of the card, beyond 'have a family, have kids, find a rainbow, have a dance'. In Kahn and Selesnick's *Carnival at the End of the World* deck, for example, a masked cowboy carries a tray with ten assorted vessels on it. Collect them and fill them as you like, is its suggestion. It's no small task, but that is the challenge at the heart of the Ten of Cups: write your own narrative. It might not be perfect, it might not look like everyone else's, and it might not be forever, but whatever it is: make it yours.

QUESTIONS TO ASK WHEN YOU SEE THIS CARD: What are you proud of? What brings you joy? Are you happy? What is the source of your happiness? Have you built the life you want? Are you comparing yourself to others? Who are your role models?

PAGE OF CUPS

INSPIRATION, DREAMS, SUBCONSCIOUS MIND, MAGIC, WONDER,
INTUITION, HIDDEN DEPTHS, CREATIVE CURIOSITY

In most tarot decks, the Page of Cups is depicted with a figure holding up a cup with a small fish in it: a little surprise, something alive and unexpected in their tableware. But in one, Marisa de la Peña's Circo Tarot, the surprise is even bigger: her Page of Cups is a giant grinning fish holding a cup with a small boy sitting inside it. This, as far as I am concerned, is the best possible visual for the Page of Cups: a card which speaks to the imagination, to the blurred lines between what is real and what isn't. It's the card of the subconscious, where myths and legends are born, and where the fantastical can come alive. (Unsurprisingly, quite a number of other decks depict this Page as a mermaid.)

The Page of Cups often signifies creative inspiration: a sudden flash of insight, an original thought. It's the moment when, after you've been turning a problem or a challenge over in the back of your mind, a solution suddenly becomes clear, like a strange creature rising from the depths of the sea and finally breaking the surface. It's the moment when you're reminded that beneath the clear-cut narrative that characterises your conscious mind, there are mysterious hidden caverns; busy workings of which you are barely aware, but which are always tinkering away at something. You see and sense far more than you realise, far more than you remember, and every sensory input is fuel thrown into the blazing furnace of your subconscious.

For that reason, the Page of Cups is strongly identified with highly creative people. But it's also powerfully associated with dreams: the weird, wonderful, and the downright peculiar products of your sleeping mind. As we all know, it can take a fair bit of combing through the detritus of your dreams before you find anything meaningful (You tattoo a moustache made of flowers onto your face! You invent a new shade of blusher and name it HAM! You find a gold coin the size of a Wagon Wheel biscuit in your pocket and give it to a rough sleeper! You ride a horse!). But the Page of Cups tells you to do it anyway, and to enjoy the process of exploring, of sifting through the fragments to see if you might strike gold. It encourages curiosity about yourself, in much the same way a therapist might, and often for similar reasons. It asks you to wonder: where did this thought come from? How do these memories fit together? What does this tell me about myself?

Indeed, it would probably be fair to say that if there was

a card that best represents the way that we read the tarot, it would be the Page of Cups. It invites you to explore and to question the stories that you tell yourself, and the stories you tell *about* yourself. It invites you to discard some of the things that you hold as unassailable truths, and consider what might happen if you listen to your dreams. It doesn't promise simple answers, but it does open the door to illumination.

QUESTIONS TO ASK WHEN YOU SEE THIS CARD: What inspires you? What have you been dreaming about lately? Has anything been recurrent? Is there anything in your life that's causing confusion right now? Are there any ideas that keep occurring to you that might seem silly but that you want to explore?

KNIGHT OF CUPS

ROMANCE, PASSION, RAW EMOTION, INSTINCT, IDEALS,
ADVENTURES, NEW RELATIONSHIPS, NEW IDEAS

The simplest way to describe the Knight of Cups is to tell you that they have *a lot of feelings*. You will have met someone like this before. You have almost certainly been this person yourself at times. If you've ever spent significant periods of time with a dog, the basic principle of the Knight of Cups will be particularly easy to grasp. They feel things deeply and they wear their heart on their sleeve. Their emotions are big: so big that they sometimes feel like they can't be contained inside a physical body.

This passion, this candour, this rawness, can be utterly

charming. This character has dreams, and they're on a mission to make them happen. But, as with all the Knights, ambition and action don't always translate into outcomes. This character is still learning, still growing, and sometimes in their enthusiasm they can make mistakes and run roughshod over other people. They don't yet have the skill of editing themself, don't always realise the ability they have to wound others. They speak from the heart, but don't necessarily engage the brain beforehand. And when they sulk, you'll know about it. Oh, you will.

This card is a depiction of the romantic in every sense of the word. It can indicate the decisive first act in a new story, one of ardent pledges, profound emotional connections, or transformative creativity. It can be about striving for new ideals, wanting to make the world a better place, and wondering at the beauty all around you. It is intuitive, driven by emotions rather than logic, and therefore it is totally irrational. When you see the Knight of Cups in a reading, know that you are dealing with the lizard brain. This is the card of the limbic system: it acts on instinct and then post-rationalises with varying degrees of success. It is the part of every person that sometimes causes them to do things which make absolutely no sense – sometimes ending in disaster, and sometimes in triumph. This card is basically most of the characters of *Moulin Rouge*, including (some might say especially) the annoying ones: everything is extra, over the top, dramatic, and deeply heartfelt.

The thing to remember is this: you cannot reason with the Knight of Cups. It is a force to be reckoned with: a deluge of emotion and passion which, once it has been set in motion, cannot be stopped. What's left to you is to try to understand how and where that force is acting. Is your querent the origin of the force, or are they in its path? And how should they respond to it? How can they? Sometimes you need to ride the wave of the Knight of Cups, let it carry you far from home and beach you on a strange new shore, for a new beginning, a new way of being. And sometimes you just have to weather it; root yourself like a rock in the surf, stand strong, and let the tide of feelings break over you. Either way, when the Knight passes through, it will leave a changed landscape in its wake.

QUESTIONS TO ASK WHEN YOU SEE THIS CARD: Does this card speak to how you're feeling? Does it remind you of anyone in your life? What big emotional currents are you caught in right now? What are your instincts telling you? How do you feel? Excited? Afraid? Safe? Unsafe?

QUEEN OF CUPS

CARE, INTUITION, PROTECTION,
EMOTIONAL INTELLIGENCE, HEALING, LOVE

The Queen of Cups is the Queen of Hearts. For better or for worse, she thinks, feels, and acts out of love. She also goes by another, more colloquial, name: she is Mum. She does not, I should point out, bear any relation to cliche stereotypes ('as a busy mum . . . '). Nor do you need to be an actual mother in the biological sense, or have one, or be talking about one to understand this card. But for most people, she conjures an idea that is familiar, regardless of how much or little it resembles your own experience of being parented. She is the primordial mother, the benevolent archetype that appears in stories from every culture. She is a concept that every mammal can understand on some bone-deep level.

As the Queen of Cups, her element is water and her emotional tank is filled with love, compassion, empathy, intuition, and possibly snacks. That risks making this card sound soft and cuddly – and she's far from it. She's got to this place because her heart has been shaped by her experiences in the world, not all of which have been straightforward and easy. Like all of the Queens, she is a mature presence in the deck, and one that speaks with authority on the energy of her suit. When you see the Queen of Cups, you're being told to respect your feelings, and the feelings of others. Does a situation make you feel uneasy? Then that's something worth exploring. Are you feeling unfulfilled? We need to do something about that.

Just by listening to yourself and others, you're channelling the best side of the Queen of Cups. You are holding space. Perhaps you're even playing that archetypal maternal role – whether that's in care for someone else, or for yourself. This Queen can be a container for your emotions. It lets you know that you can show and share your feelings, that they are taken seriously. That you are seen and heard, and not judged. This is a card about tapping into your feelings and your emotional intelligence, and intuiting the way, whether you're trying to overcome an obstacle, or choosing a new career path, or helping a friend. And when it appears in a reading, it can ask you to check in on whether you are offering yourself the gentleness and love that you need – or whether you are receiving that care from the people around you.

This card also makes me think of a lesson shared by the author Jeanette Winterson, who wrote about her traumatic childhood with her adoptive parents (specifically her 'monster' mother) in her memoir *Why Be Happy When You Could Be Normal?* Later on in life, she reconciled with her adoptive father. 'When I look at my life I realise that the mistakes I have made, the things I really regret, were not errors of judgement but failures of feeling,' she wrote on her blog after his death. She urged others who are estranged from or fighting with significant figures in their lives to 'try and find the emotional space, gently, gradually, without force or artifice, to start to repair the damage'. This appeal to connection and understanding as a way of healing yourself is what lies at the heart of the Queen of Cups.

QUESTIONS TO ASK WHEN YOU SEE THIS CARD: Are you listening to yourself? Do you trust your intuition? Do you feel seen by those around you? Who cares for you, and for whom do you care? What might empathy repair for you?

KING OF CUPS

SELF-KNOWLEDGE, EMPATHY, COMPASSION, PATIENCE,
VALIDATION, MANIPULATION

A King of Cups is attuned to the needs of their heart, but they aren't governed by it. They're not impervious to the highs, lows, and occasional tiger pits of the emotions: they just don't allow them to trip them up. When a feeling comes up, even if it's one they weren't expecting, they greet it like an old friend. Hello anger, hello joy, hi sadness and suspicion, and good day to you, lust. This King exhibits a degree of emotional stability that is rarely encountered in day-to-day life. And when it appears in a reading, it's asking a querent to consider the extent of their ability to master their own heart, and at whose knee they learnt to do so.

None of the figures of the tarot are tied to a specific gender. But here, in the suit that so often speaks to family, it's hard to see this card and not think about father figures – whether strictly biological, found fathers, or symbolic ones. This King asks us to think about those benevolent paternal characters: people in whom we trust, and whose influence on our lives has been gentle, instructive, and emotionally open. For me, it invites memories of my grandfather: a man who had spent his career in the military, but who hadn't let it make him cold or distant. When someone did wrong by him, he would consider the matter and, usually, his response was simply to say, 'That was unthinking.' He didn't ask others to repress their feelings, and he wasn't in thrall to his own. He taught me the difficult business of acting with care and compassion.

Like all of the Kings, though, this card is double-edged. Anyone who is so able to master their emotions must acknowledge the influence they have over others, and the duty they have to model the right behaviours. Father figures can be problematic: they have power that can all too easily be abused. This is a dynamic that plays out in many situations beyond the domestic: you see it again and again in professional environments, in politics, in the media. For me, Katherine Angel perfectly captures the gift and the challenge of the King of Cups in her writing about this dynamic in *Daddy Issues*: 'Creating the capacity for love is the hardest thing a parent has to do, and it is hard for parents to do it if they need love from the child in order to feel themselves to be real.' At their best, a King of Cups recognises when to step back from the furnace of their own feelings in order to help someone else grow into their own. But when they use their influence to demand that their own needs be prioritised, they can suffocate the emotional lives of those whom they ought to be nurturing.

This card represents emotional intelligence of the highest order: not a destination but a life's work. When the King of Cups appears, it's a moment to think about what it means to step into your power and be the bigger person. Not in a martyred, or self-congratulatory sense, but in the sense of knowing when you have the upper hand in a dynamic, and handling yourself accordingly.

QUESTIONS TO ASK WHEN YOU SEE THIS CARD: How do you handle your emotions? When do you rule them, and when do they rule you? Do you use them to bring about positive change, or do you expect others to attend to them for you? Have you been the recipient of compassionate leadership? Or have you been manipulated?

CHAPTER 5

The Pentacles

The Pentacles are often referred to or renamed as Coins, and accordingly are sometimes assumed to be all about the CASH CASH MONEY MONEY. There's a fairly prosaic explanation for this, which is that they look like coins. Pentacles are large, flat golden discs with five-pointed stars etched into their surfaces. They aren't coins, though, and what they represent is far broader than finances.

The Pentacles' element is earth. It is the most solid of the suits, and the slowest. These cards do not deal in spontaneity: there is no caprice and precious little whimsy to be found here. They are a grounding force in the tarot, very much rooted in the physical world, and they always deal with what you can have and hold: the things you can literally touch. They speak to the home, the body, and possessions. With the Pentacles, we're often right at the bottom of Maslow's hierarchy of needs, in the physiological requirements. So when these cards appear, they invite you to consider your material well-being: your health, your professional life, your living situation and, yes, sometimes your bank balance. The Pentacles ask that age-old question: how solid are your foundations? Where do your resources flow to and from?

You'll quickly see that the Pentacles offer up a trove of

topics for a querent. Security, stability and safety are recurring themes in the suit, as are their opposites. Teamwork and generosity are here, and so are avarice and hoarding. Fairness and lack thereof makes a solid appearance halfway through. Comfort and richness sit cheek by jowl with isolation and exclusion. And up in the court cards, a strong case is made for keeping on top of your admin. It might not seem like the wildest ride, but it's an important one, and it covers a great deal of ground – much more than you might realise at first.

Indeed, it's impossible to ignore the fact that, in raising questions about *have* and *have-not*, the Pentacles are cards that often speak to political issues. The society we exist in has a particular shape. It has finite resources that are unequally shared; it has privilege and poverty, victors and victims. Many people find that this is the suit which creates the most opportunities to acknowledge, articulate, and explore the structural realities that govern their experience of living in the world. It's also the suit that can best speak to the power of community, and the ways in which groups of people can support one another.

The Pentacles might be the cards which seem the most fixed, but that doesn't mean that they don't create opportunities for change. The earth isn't just cold, eternal stone. It is fertile ground, a slumbering powerhouse for metamorphosis. This is the suit of growing things: of plants and flowers, trees and forests. And if there's one thing that plants know, it's that nothing is ever born from nothing. New growth must be fed and nurtured, and it can be slow. Nobody ever said photosynthesis was easy – turning sunlight into matter is, arguably, the closest real thing we've got to magic. It is a steady and remarkable act of transformation that creates things we can *touch*; things that can endure for centuries; things that can heal their own wounds and keep on going, reshaping themselves to better thrive in their changing environments.

Some people find these cards, which deal with the material world, less exciting than other parts of the deck. What you need to hold in your mind when reading these cards is that pentacles aren't simply objects: they're talismans. They are imbued with magical power, the seeds of change. Each one creates opportunities to consider how and where you might have the power to transform things – real things – for the better.

ACE OF PENTACLES

MATERIAL CHANGES, NEW CIRCUMSTANCES, OPPORTUNITIES,
CONSEQUENCES, FAILURE, FEAR

The Aces of the tarot are all about beginnings, with the particular nature of that beginning tied to the element and energy of the suit – in this case, earth, and the physical world. In its most literal interpretations, then, the Ace of Pentacles is a card about material opportunities and changes. It could be obvious: moving house or starting a new job. Or it could be more subtle: shifting circumstances, a physical change in your body, reaching a new phase in your life. The Ace asks you what's on your horizon: what is about to be manifested and made real, by your own efforts or otherwise?

It goes without saying that there is extraordinary power

and potential in this card. But the thing I like most about it is how it speaks to the fact that not all new beginnings are huge, earth-shaking ones. The grand gestures and seismic shifts of the tarot largely live in the Major Arcana. The Ace of Pentacles, by comparison, deals with the importance of even the most everyday decisions and changes. It acknowledges that there are things that many or most people will experience in the course of their lives, but which don't have any less impact on them for being commonplace. Millions of people will move, change jobs, retire, enter puberty or the menopause, become a parent, grandparent, aunt, uncle, or sibling in any given year – life runs in endless cycles of budding, blossoming, fruiting, and falling. But events don't have to be rare to be important. Sometimes changes are wanted, needed, or expected; sometimes they are disruptive, to be resisted or endured; sometimes they are wonderful surprises. And, of course, there's no telling what the long-term consequences of any of them might be.

Naturally, most depictions of this card feature one very large golden pentacle. Often, it is cupped in the palm of a hand in the foreground of a largely empty landscape. The way that it's held, and the context in which it's seen, recalls a seed ready to be sowed. That, for me, is the best way to think of this Ace. It represents the moment of planting, and the potential for germination. It doesn't guarantee any outcome, but it does allow you to wonder what might happen if this fragment of life were to take root and grow. Perhaps a rare and delicate flower will emerge, or perhaps just a common weed. And perhaps it won't take – if the soil isn't quite right, or the weather is too harsh, or the seed needs to sleep for a little longer before it sprouts. Regardless of what happens, there is something wondrous in its unknown potential, and in giving it the chance to be realised.

We all know the phrase about great oaks and little acorns,

but the words that most often come to mind when I see this card are from a poem by Angela Carter: 'The smallest things are not the least marvellous.' When something new comes into the world, no matter how small, it opens up the possibility of marvels. The consequences might be the tiniest ripples, or far greater than we could imagine. But the outcome isn't what matters. What matters is being bold enough to try.

QUESTIONS TO ASK WHEN YOU SEE THIS CARD: What changes are on the horizon for you? What do you want to do and realise in the world? What small action could you take to begin something new? What consequences do you hope for, and what are you afraid of?

TWO OF PENTACLES

COMPETING PRIORITIES, BALANCE, IMBALANCE,
DISORGANISATION, STRESS

The Two of Pentacles is usually depicted with a figure standing on the shore of the sea, juggling two pentacles like a circus performer. Sometimes, you look at this card and think: how fabulous. Look at how this person juggles those discs; what flow and what style. At other times, you look and think . . . hmm, a little wobbly: I sense jeopardy here. How a querent responds to the card matters, because it says a lot about how they're feeling right now.

This is a card of being busy: of juggling life's many competing responsibilities. It refers to anything that requires practical attention and action: keeping plates spinning at work; managing finances, schedules, family members; locating and wearing same-pair shoes; even just maintaining basic levels of personal hygiene. When this card appears, it offers a chance to check in with how you're doing at your own personal juggling act. Sometimes you have that elusive 'flow' and clear the high-jump of daily life with many inches to spare. That's a magical feeling, and one that ought to be appreciated if it reflects your reality. But this card can also speak to those times when you feel like you keep on clipping the bar – or crashing into it entirely.

The difference between the two can be an incredibly sensitive topic – and one which feels perilously close to a personal judgement. When I see this card, I think of something Tina Fey wrote about being a working mother in her memoir *Bossypants*. She explains that the rudest question you can ask a woman isn't 'How old are you?' or 'What do you weigh?' but 'How do you juggle it all?' Because the implication is that you're performing some kind of party trick, and that you won't be able to forever. And the worst bit is, that is often exactly how it feels. You are, indeed, juggling, and, no, not at all perfectly – not that you need it pointed out to you.

When you're in the thick of it, it doesn't help to have your performance evaluated: you've just got to keep it going. You've got to master some pretty nifty footwork to keep everything up in the air when the waves come crashing in. What you don't need is someone watching you, commenting on you, making noise, or, god forbid, more work. You need someone to acknowledge you, to see that this isn't easy, to understand what it's like to be juggling on shifting sands and to – dare we say it – offer to help.

The Two of Pentacles knows this. It's a card, so ultimately it can't do your tax return or the laundry or pick up a sick child from nursery on your behalf, but what it can do is see you. This card hasn't appeared to throw you off balance with its incessant questions or clueless observations. It has appeared to acknowledge that you've got a lot going on and that, even if you're making it look easy, it's probably not. Honest and open communication is the key here. This card reminds you that, when you see someone juggling (especially if that person is you), it's time to put ego aside and really listen to what's needed.

QUESTIONS TO ASK WHEN YOU SEE THIS CARD: Where are you right now? Do you feel like you're juggling everything? Is this a time for listening or talking? How would you like to be supported?

THREE OF PENTACLES

TEAMWORK, COLLABORATION, CO-OPERATION, ASKING FOR HELP,
SHARING THE LOAD, TRYING TO DO TOO MUCH ALONE

After the balancing act of the previous card, the Three of
Pentacles arrives with some welcome news: help is at hand.
In the Rider Waite Smith deck, this is illustrated with three
figures who are building a cathedral. This is, famously, rather
an ambitious architectural project, but the point of this card
isn't scale: it's collaboration. No single person could build a
cathedral on their own: they need others who will also work
to the best of their abilities. This is the card of teamwork, of
sharing the load. It says that the whole is greater than the sum
of its parts and it speaks to the ways people come together to

get a job done. There's only one way to build a cathedral: brick by brick.

We have an unhelpful myth as a society that successful people are individuals who are gifted and talented: that they've done it all by themselves. This isn't just unhelpful; it's misleading. In *Outliers*, Malcolm Gladwell concludes that success is never the result of a solo effort. 'No one,' he says, 'not rock stars, not professional athletes, not software billionaires, and not even geniuses – ever makes it alone.' When you see this card, you're being asked to think about the ways in which you work with others to achieve a goal or get things done. These goals don't have to be lofty, necessarily: maybe it's getting a weekly shop so you have food in your fridge, or updating your CV. Or maybe it is something huge: maybe you're building your metaphorical cathedral; the great work of your lifetime. Either way, the Three of Pentacles speaks to the fact that very few projects aren't improved by another pair of eyes or another pair of hands. Learning from others, and working together towards a common goal, is something worth celebrating.

This card can also be a reminder that it's alright to ask for help. It's impossible for me to see this card and not think about what it was like to become a mother in a global lockdown: to have been a small and precious creature's entire world; their love, comfort, food, and entertainment – and them, yours. And while that situation might be fine for some, even preferable in those earliest months, it's not sustainable – or in anyone's best interests – in the long term. It takes a village to raise a child, they say. That's true. In fact, almost anything that needs to be raised, built, or grown benefits from collaboration.

When you see this card, it's an opportunity to explore how (and if) you let others into your life, your work, and your ambitions. It can ask you to consider collaborating with someone else on a project or asking for mentorship and opportunities to learn from others – or even just for someone else to hold the baby so you can rest your arms for a while. It doesn't matter what task you're faced with or what challenge life has thrown at you. What matters is that you'll be more likely to succeed at it if you bring in other people.

QUESTIONS TO ASK WHEN YOU SEE THIS CARD: What goal are you trying to achieve and who could help you get there? What are your strengths? What are your weaknesses? How might you collaborate or ask others for help? Do you struggle to ask for help?

FOUR OF PENTACLES

STABILITY, SECURITY, SAFETY, CONSERVATISM, SAVING,
SELF-PROTECTION, FEARFULNESS, STAGNATION, PARALYSIS

The traditional depiction of this card is a little king, in a little city. He has a nice little crown, a nice little throne, and four very nice little pentacles. All in all, he's doing quite well for himself in his nice little world. It's balanced, firm, and solid, with a low centre of gravity. Four is a good number of pentacles to have. It's stable. Like a table. The Four of Pentacles is a stable table.

When it appears in a reading, this Four brings up questions about security: specifically, do you have it? Do you need it? What do you need to do to ensure it? Having a safety net is never a bad idea. There are times in life when the music suddenly stops and you need to sit down; when you need to hold your place while you focus on something else; or even when you need to brace for impact. There are times when you don't need perfect, you just need good enough: a warm berth in a storm, a place to rest, or perhaps to lick your wounds, recuperate, and rally your strength. And there are times when it's just really nice to feel like you've got your shit together, and you want to try to keep it that way for a while. The Four of Pentacles sees you and invites you to do that if it's what you need.

But it also asks: what happens when sitting down becomes the norm? What happens when your safety net stops being the thing that will catch you if you fall, and starts being where you live? What happens when you put all of your energy into squirrelling things away for the future, and never allow yourself to live in the present? The answer is nothing. Nothing happens. Nothing ever will.

Because the thing is that stable tables don't have much in the way of adventure. They have very little forward momentum (and by very little, I mean . . . none). This is a perfectly acceptable landscape, but it won't change, and nothing new can grow here. The Four of Pentacles offers security, but it also reminds us that there's a moment when safe becomes stagnant, when pause becomes paralysis, and when standing still becomes avoiding movement. It invites you to think about the things you're not doing and the risks that seem too big right now. It asks you to examine whether they really are out of reach and when, exactly, you'll be ready to see security not just as a safety net, but as a springboard for action?

The Four of Pentacles is a traveller's way-stop on your journey, not the ultimate destination. It's a cosy hut in which you can hide from the rain; a chance to regroup, take stock, and shore up your defences. But it's also the kind of place where, if you stay too long, you'll begin to feel the walls closing in. This card should remind you that while it might feel like a risk to exchange a pleasant and predictable place of shelter for the wild unknown, often the real trap lies in staying put. It isn't a call for radical upheaval, but it is a reminder to open the door and see what lies beyond your four walls.

QUESTIONS TO ASK WHEN YOU SEE THIS CARD: Do you feel like you have enough of a safety net? Have you been standing still for too long? Is there a part of your life which is stagnating? What's holding you back from taking the next step?

FIVE OF PENTACLES

EXCLUSION, ISOLATION, LONELINESS, DISCRIMINATION,
OSTRACISATION, OTHERING, CHOICE

The Five of Pentacles is not an easy card in the tarot. This is the card of isolation, exclusion, even ostracisation. It isn't about healthy sequestering and introspection, or taking a step back from the world to centre yourself. It's a card of profound loneliness. Its depictions vary quite wildly between decks but, generally, it's an illustration of poverty. In the Rider Waite Smith, the image is literal, and useful to know: two people, hunched and ragged, stand in the snow outside a softly glowing church window. The contrast between their situation and that of the unseen congregation inside is stark. For some reason, the figures on this card aren't welcome in a space that is supposedly open to all.

This card speaks to the ways in which you can feel vulnerable, and alone: the moments when you seem to be missing out on things that everyone else takes for granted. The heart of this card is the acknowledgement that sometimes there are experiences which are painfully unavailable to you: whether it's career success, finding love, being well in mind or body, having a place to call home, or someone with whom to spend Christmas. It can indicate a difficult period of time for a querent – sometimes past, sometimes present.

The thing you don't have doesn't even have to be something you long for. As I know very well, being the only single, childless person in a group of friends, for example, can be unsettling and lonely, even when you are happily unattached. We all have a powerful instinct to do as others do, and tensions can arise when, for whatever reason, someone doesn't. It shouldn't be that way, but it is. Sheila Heti speaks to this in *Motherhood*: 'One person's life is not a political or general statement about how all lives should be. Other lives should be able to exist alongside our own without any threat or judgment at all'. It can feel as though, if you take a different path to those around you, you have to justify the arc of your story before you've even experienced it – and to do so with far more conviction that it's the right decision than you could possibly have.

It's also impossible to ignore this card's relationship to bigger topics. The Five recognises that structural inequalities exist and that they have a powerful, material impact on people's experiences of the world. Your gender, the colour of your skin, your age, who you love, the way your body works and looks, the way your mind functions, and a thousand other things besides, influence whether society allows you to feel that you belong. This card speaks to both micro-aggressions and overt acts of exclusion and prejudice: lived experiences that shape lives. When it appears, it is worth exploring how belonging and not-belonging manifests in your life: where do you experience exclusion? Where, perhaps, do you perpetuate it for others?

The Fives in the tarot are all about imbalances and discomfort. They are generally cards of reflection, rather than action: these are moments and experiences from which you can't simply extract yourself; which must be acknowledged for what they are. Perhaps it is within your power to remedy feeling lonely or excluded, or perhaps (more likely) it's not. Regardless, the Five of Pentacles tells you that it's important to notice the feeling, and what it means to you.

QUESTIONS TO ASK WHEN YOU SEE THIS CARD: Where do you feel like you belong? Do you feel excluded or isolated from something? Do you feel left behind? Is there something other people have that you can't?

SIX OF PENTACLES

SUPPORT, ASSISTANCE, NEED, POWER, INEQUALITY,
GENEROSITY, ATTENTION, SELF-CARE

When my son was very young, we taught him that it's nice to share. In true toddler fashion, he initially just took this to mean that he should just shout 'SHARE' when taking what he wanted – a toy, a biscuit, our dog's ball – from whoever had it. It took time for him to learn that sharing was a two-way street: that he had resources which he could choose to keep for himself or give to others, and that the latter path was, from time to time, the better option for everyone. Eventually, he realised that everything could be shared and, for a time, everything was – and quite emphatically, too: turns on the swing, shoes with friends, dinner with the dog. Sharing might be a lesson first received when we're very young, but it can take decades to fully understand it. 'To share' means more than just 'to give'. It's about doing the right thing, and doing it fairly. It means learning that, when things are uneven, you don't have to accept it – you can get up and do something about it.

That's the lesson at the heart of this card. The Six of Pentacles speaks to acts of generosity, and the distribution of resources. It's traditionally known as the charity card – but to today's reader, it might better be thought of in terms of mutual aid: individuals and communities coming together to support one another and to address the structures that are causing a problem, rather than just a linear flow of resources. And, while it can be interpreted as financial aid, it really speaks to support in the broadest of senses. It represents practical help, a generosity of spirit or care. It's donating regularly to causes you believe in, checking in on a neighbour, or stepping in to advocate for someone who is being treated unfairly. It's telling someone you love them without needing to hear it back. It can be a reminder of the value of offering what we have to those who need it – whether that's money, time, attention, or privilege. And, of course, it also speaks to being able to accept whatever form of help you need when it's offered to you.

This can be a very positive card indeed. When you see or experience pain, injustice, inequality, or exclusion, as happens in the Five of Pentacles, it can feel stultifying and impossible to alter. What could one single voice possibly do? Who would hear you? Yet, with the Six, you can find yourself being spurred into action. This card is a reminder that you don't need bottomless pockets, or to solve all the world's ills in a single stroke. Meaningful change can come in increments, through regular effort – one voice added to another can start a revolution. This Six speaks to all of the choices we make, no matter how small, about how we spend our resources – whether that's about what we buy, the media we consume, or just the causes and people to which we offer our attention.

Of course, as my son (now) knows very well, the best sort of sharing involves reciprocity – not necessarily immediately, but certainly in the long term. There are times when, after a period of needing aid, the balance shifts, and you find yourself able to give. The Six also reminds us of the value of knowing when it's time to pay those acts of generosity forward.

QUESTIONS TO ASK WHEN YOU SEE THIS CARD: Do you know how to ask for help? Do you have the resources, personally or financially, to help others? What one thing can you change today to affect the world around you positively?

SEVEN OF PENTACLES

EFFORT, HARD WORK, REFLECTION, PERSPECTIVE,
ADJUSTING YOUR PATH

The tarot is too old to know memes and yet sometimes, inadvertently, it does them. And it does them very well indeed. Cast your mind back to the start of the suit and the Ace of Pentacles: the seed of possibility being planted in the earth. Between the Ace and the Seven of Pentacles, that seed has had time to either germinate and flourish or wither and die. Between then and now, we have: how it started... and how it's going.

And on the surface of things, it's going WELL. The sort of well that would allow you to post satisfying before and after photos on social media. But at the heart of both the tarot card and the meme lies a valuable lesson: that just because you haven't yet reached the end point of what you're doing, it doesn't mean you can't stop to evaluate your progress. The Rider Waite Smith deck depicts this idea, as it does so often in this suit, through a gardening metaphor: a figure leans on a hoe as they look at a bush they have been tending. Pentacle-flowers bloom in abundance on the bush but the look on the person's face isn't joyous, it's pensive. There is no thought bubble above their head, but their mind isn't too hard to read – it's full of questions. Was this bush meant to be this big? What are these bizarre fruits? Is this... a money tree? Is it witchcraft? Should I burn it or plant another?

The Seven of Pentacles marks a turning point in the suit when you get to step back from the easel of life and decide whether you like the way the painting is turning out. It can prompt conversations about specific decisions: about work, say, or whether or not it's a good idea to keep climbing this mountain in the sweltering heat on the last day of your holiday in Indonesia (it was not, but I did it anyway). It could also be a broader 'how are things going?' A relationship, for example, or the general trajectory of this decade of your life. It's a chance to ask yourself: is this what you thought it would be and, if it's not, do you like it? Is the path you've chosen still one that serves you? Have you underestimated how demanding or costly or time-consuming or rewarding your pursuits would be? Do you need to keep on keeping on, or have a serious conversation with yourself? Were sandals the right choice of footwear for this ascent?

The gift of this card is in realising that your power doesn't lie in struggling across a finish line for the sake of it. It lies in making the right choice for yourself, even if that means stopping. Of course it's nice to have a finished product, a goal achieved, or a milestone reached, but you're also not a robotic arm on a factory assembly line. You can say no! Changing your mind and your direction, making minor adjustments to your path – or major ones – are just as valid as seeing something through to the end. The Seven of Pentacles doesn't tell you you have to put something down. But it does tell you that it's totally fine to do that, if that's what you want.

QUESTIONS TO ASK WHEN YOU SEE THIS CARD: So, how's that thing going? Are you happy with the results so far? Does success feel the way you imagined it would? What's working for you? What's not? Do you need to change your approach? Do you need to stop?

EIGHT OF PENTACLES

ROUTINE, REPETITION, PERSEVERANCE, SATISFACTION,
BOREDOM, PROCRASTINATION

There's a question that I like to ask people I work with: 'are you a HUSKY or are you a WHIPPET?' None of my colleagues are dogs, sadly, but the question is a metaphor: it's about how you do your job best. Some people are like huskies, who love nothing more than to set a solid pace and run, on and on, smiling the whole way, matching their step to the team and burning through the miles. Others are like whippets, in that they prefer to be asleep for approximately twenty-three hours a day, and then just absolutely leg it for one short, chaotic – but terrifyingly effective – burst of energy. There's technically no right answer, but when this card appears, it's likely to feel familiar to the people who give one response, and deeply uncomfortable to those who give the other.

The Eight of Pentacles, in this analogy, is about when you need to be a husky, not a whippet. This is the card of finding joy and satisfaction in routine, repetition, and process. The Germans, as is often the case, have a very good word for this sort of thing: *sitzfleich*, which is literally the power to sit on your bum and get things done. The Eight is usually depicted as a craftsman making identical pentacles, one by one. He's not trying to innovate on the form or experimenting with different techniques and styles, but he is learning, improving, growing, and developing through process. He's making a series of matched objects, and he's doing it because he must. Someone has to hammer out those pentacles and, today, that someone is him – so he's damn well going to make them the best they can be.

There are, of course, many aspects of life to which this visual metaphor is applicable. Your actual job, for a start: for almost everyone in the world, a significant part of professional life involves doing the same kind of things over and over. It might be uneventful, even tedious, but it's how you get paid, get results, and improve. This card is also a reminder of the other places in life where repetition and routine are beneficial. Health is clearly relevant here: regular sleep, meals, and movement might not be the most exciting things in the world, but they do go a long way to keeping you feeling well. For a long time, I resisted the notion that exercise creates immediate endorphin highs but, in my thirties, have come to grudgingly admit that regularly doing something resembling a workout does make me feel a little bit better overall.

And that's the thing about the Eight of Pentacles. This is not a card of marvels and highs and wonders. It doesn't promise excitement. It offers satisfaction: the feeling of contentment that comes from a job well done and the joy of practicing your craft. It's a day spent happily pulling your metaphorical dog-sled and keeping promises to yourself about the things you want to do. At its best, it opens the way to progress – perhaps even mastery. And, even if the task at hand isn't one that you care about for its own sake, the Eight of Pentacles asks if you might not find a way to appreciate the ability to do it well.

QUESTIONS TO ASK WHEN YOU SEE THIS CARD: Are you giving enough time and care to your work? Are you procrastinating and doing rush jobs? Do you need more routine in your life? Do you feel bored by what you're doing, or is there a way to find satisfaction in it?

NINE OF PENTACLES

INDEPENDENCE, AUTONOMY, SELF-RELIANCE, LUXURY, PRIDE,
SEXUALITY, SUCCESS, AVOIDANCE, FEAR OF INTIMACY

To me, the Nine of Pentacles is first and foremost the patron saint of the happy singleton. And that means that she is Cher. More specifically, she is Cher giving the infamous interview in which she is asked about her relationships. She answers with an anecdote: 'My mom said to me, You know, sweetheart, one day you should settle down and marry a rich man. And I said, Mom – I am a rich man.' This Nine is a woman who stands in her own power. She is a Rich Man. Sometimes that's literal: this card can speak to professional and financial success. The crucial point is that her motivation comes from within.

Her achievements are things that she has worked for or built because she wanted to, not because someone told her she must.

Because she's ruled by the Pentacles, she also asks us to consider satisfaction and autonomy of the body. She has, to quote Tess McGill in *Working Girl*, 'a head for business and a bod for sin.' She's an earthy, sensual character who doesn't confuse sex with emotions; who is confident enough in herself and what she wants that she can take lovers without always falling in love. As Cher says, 'I love men – I think men are the coolest. But you don't really need them to live.' This is true of romantic and sexual partners of all genders: the Nine of Pentacles knows that there's a difference between wanting people and needing them. There's something extraordinary in this self-reliance, this not being beholden to anyone or anything; the ability to do what you want, when you want, and how you want. And, while there has always been a certain amount of societal disapproval of women who choose to live independently (men, not so much), it's hard not to understand the appeal.

Of course, you don't have to be literally embracing the single life to appreciate the bounty of the Nine of Pentacles. This card invites you to notice the spaces and places in your life in which you create your own richness. What have you achieved? What has your work earned you? Sometimes, it's a card that can be a much-needed reminder that you – yes, you! – are enough. This is a party for one. You don't need other people's approval and validation to feel pleased with what you do and who you are. You are allowed to carve out space in your life to do the things that bring you satisfaction and fulfilment. And you are allowed to tell people who try to stop you, who suggest ways you might change yourself, or who try to make you smaller and lesser than you are, to go away and leave you alone.

The shadow truth of this card, which occasionally reveals itself in a reading, is also worth remembering. It's that sometimes, when you *can* do everything alone, you end up feeling like you *should* do everything alone. And, of course, you needn't. The Nine can be a reminder to check in with the soft animal parts of yourself. Has your luxurious pelt become a suit of gleaming armour designed not to invite caresses, but to keep the rest of the world at bay? Remember that you're allowed to reach out a hand. You're allowed to be vulnerable. No man is an island, not even a rich one.

QUESTIONS TO ASK WHEN YOU SEE THIS CARD: Are you comfortable being alone? Do you value independence? Are you self-reliant? What are you proud of? What are your successes? Are you able to create space for yourself? Do you have avoidant tendencies?

TEN OF PENTACLES

Jen and I are very, very good at moving house. We're both from military families and, as children, every couple of years we'd find ourselves in new towns, or even new countries, with everything familiar left behind. We ghosted in and out of schools – there are probably dozens of class photographs out there with our faces in, unrecognisable and unremembered by the people we once stood beside in matching uniforms. We also both had parents who had grown up the same way and who, even as adults, had never known what it meant to have a fixed geographical place in the world. It's a disorienting lifestyle for any child, and a hard one to support them through. After a particularly unhappy move, I remember asking my mother, where is home? Why can't we have a home? She replied, 'We do have a home. We just don't know where we're going to put it yet.'

The ability to create safe spaces for ourselves is at the heart of the Ten of Pentacles. When we see the Tens in the tarot, we're promised completion, and with the Pentacles, that completion is meant to offer us security: domestic, familial, professional, financial. This card, more or less, signifies the idea of Home. For those who didn't have bizarrely itinerant childhoods, i.e. most people, it tends to immediately recall a specific location; something built of bricks and mortar; a place full of memories and possessions that ground you in yourself. But to read this card only as representing physical spaces is to miss out on its most beautiful gift. Buildings change hands, their foundations can crack and crumble, they can decline into dust and neglect. Even the things that appear to be most substantial, and to which we anchor ourselves, are rarely indestructible.

When this card appears, it can speak to material security but what it really asks is what you need to feel safe and secure. It raises the question of how you cultivate that inner sense of a home – the one that allowed my mother to cope with, perhaps even enjoy, moving from country to country. Growing up, Jen and I always envied the solidity of other people's homes, the certainty of being from a place, and having history there. Now we wonder if perhaps those early years – bewildering though they were – prepared us both quite well for the shifting sands of adulthood.

The Ten of Pentacles is a reminder that home doesn't need to be a permanent structure, nor does it have to stay the same over the years. It's something that you carry with you. Maybe you do that literally: a photo album, a grandmother's ring, a family, a bird feeder on a window. And maybe you do it metaphorically, holding on to a place of safety that you've created for yourself: a treasured memory, an imagined garden that grows and changes as you grow and change, too. A place where you sow seeds in the cracks on the stone stairs to soften them and invite other people in, a haven from which you can venture out into the world. This card is a reminder that, if you make your truest home inside yourself, you can take it wherever you want.

QUESTIONS TO ASK WHEN YOU SEE THIS CARD. What does home mean to you? Where do you feel safe? Do you have a home right now, or do you feel unmoored? How do you ground yourself? Could you centre your security within yourself?

PAGE OF PENTACLES

LEARNING AND DEVELOPMENT, OPTIMISM, OPEN-MINDEDNESS,
LACK OF FOCUS, LACK OF EXPERIENCE

HI THERE! It's the Page of Pentacles, your bouncy intern, arriving for work at 8.05am, despite no one else getting into the office until 9.30. Is there anything you need doing? Some post you need me to open? A coffee run, perhaps? Or maybe you'd like me to do your job for you? I'd be so happy to!! Who knows? Maybe one day I'll run the company.

Welcome to the Page of Pentacles. They're earnest, keen, and diligent, but also a bit of a daydreamer. Tell them about a project you're working on and their eyes will widen as they imagine all of the possibilities it presents. They don't want a job, they want a vocation, and what they lack in experience they more than make up for with energy. This Page is a doer, god love 'em, and even if they don't get everything right the first time, they know that by taking on any jobs thrown their way, they'll get somewhere. If a pentacle is the seed of an idea, then this Page is its most attentive gardener. When they're given one, they hold it up high for it to glimmer in the sun. To you it might be small change, but for them it's imbued with infinite potential, and they take care to notice its shine, its texture, its surface. And once it's buried in the earth, they'll tend it carefully while it discovers what it might become.

All of the Pages in the tarot have the wide-eyed enthusiasm that we commonly associate with youth. It's easy to raise an eyebrow at them but, really, the world doesn't need any more cynics. The Page of Pentacles is intuitive and acts accordingly in all things: the relationships in their life, the practical matters of work, their home and health. They represent the joy in trying something new, of putting yourself out there, of saying 'yes' and seeing where things lead. They're creative, imaginative, and, being an earth card, also very sensual. They know that it's good to slow down, to truly observe your environment, to notice the daisies in the grass, to see the clouds in the sky and feel the sun on your skin. It's almost impossible to hate this kind of energy in your life. And couldn't we all do with having a bit more of it?

Whether this card represents a person or state of mind, when it arrives in a reading, it's an invitation to examine your relationship with the material world. Do you like where you live? Does your career excite you? How do you feel in your body? The Page isn't interested in following rational and conventional approaches, or caring about what others think and about how things are supposed to go. Instead, they follow their gut. That attitude can be frustrating at times – as it is with any beginner who doesn't know the ropes yet. But it can also lead to the most extraordinary insights, and open up new avenues to explore. So maybe it's time to follow that lead a little. Put yourself out there, try something new, and don't make assumptions about where it will take you.

QUESTIONS TO ASK WHEN YOU SEE THIS CARD: What do you want from life? What is the first step you could take to get closer to that goal? Are you feeling jaded? Are you feeling inspired? What excites you? What does your instinct tell you?

KNIGHT OF PENTACLES

STRUCTURE, DILIGENCE, PRACTICALITY, RELIABILITY,
TRUSTWORTHINESS, PERFECTIONISM, DULLNESS

The Knights of the tarot are the embodiment of what happens when you take the energy of each suit to its extreme. And what do you get when you push earth – solid, grounding, slow – to its logical conclusion? You get boring, that's what. So hello, and let's give a warm welcome to the Knight of Pentacles. He's dull! He's dependable! And he's fine with that!!

What's nice about the Knight of Pentacles is that you get to be fine with that too. This Knight is going nowhere fast, and every step of the way is carefully planned, methodical, and cautiously executed. It's a rare person who aspires to be more like this, but it's also a rare person who doesn't need to from time to time. You can't always cling on by your fingertips, wing it, and hope for the best. You can't always have your head in the clouds. Sometimes you need to burst your own bubble and come back down to earth. Feel that nice solid ground beneath your feet? That's called DILIGENCE. It's called paying attention, crossing the *I*s and dotting the *T*s. It's called work. It's called being reliable.

The Knight of Pentacles is the person – or the part of you – who does not screw things up. They don't forget to answer emails, miss appointments, or let deadlines fly by unnoticed. They remember passwords, and have an excellent credit score because they always pay bills on time. They know how to say no to things that are going to interfere with their ability to show up for the important parts of their life. This is someone who can be trusted to look after others: you can leave your child or your pet with them, and know that when you return, they'll be well-fed and well-cared for. The Knight of Pentacles isn't the life and soul of the party, but they're on hand to help you pick glitter off the countertops afterwards, no matter how long it takes. (And you know it takes forever.)

When this Knight appears, it's a moment to check in with how well you're doing on, well, admin. Are you on top of it, or is it getting out of hand? And if it is, who can you learn from to make it better? What structures can you put in place to help yourself? Our own most apt illustration of this card relates to financial matters. One of these authors, who shall remain anonymous, has for several years in a row caused the other one no small degree of consternation with her slapdash and chaotic approach to doing the company tax return. The recurrent theme of January had been panicked phone calls, and it was high time to summon the inner Knight of Pentacles. And now:

there are spreadsheets! There are records of passwords! The admin prince walks among us.

Of course, while there's no such thing as being too reliable or too dependable, there is such a thing as being too dull. This Knight usually invites you to consider how and if you're showing up for yourself and others and whether you're bringing the right kind of practical energy to the world. But it can also appear when someone needs to lighten up a little (hello, perfectionists). If that's you, take the hint.

QUESTIONS TO ASK WHEN YOU SEE THIS CARD: Are you on top of things? Can you be depended upon by yourself and others? What structure and practices would help you to achieve what you need to? Where do you need to be more diligent? Where can you be less conservative, less cautious, less stuck?

QUEEN OF PENTACLES

BEAUTY, SENSATION, MENTORSHIP, CONSUMERISM,
OVERINDULGENCE, SELF-DENIAL, TREATS, DECADENCE

In the most traditional interpretations of the tarot, the Queen of Pentacles has a benevolent but somewhat uninspiring reputation. This character is safe and solid, a warm cocoon and a nurturing, reassuring presence who's good at practical things – if any of the Queens could build you a bookcase, it's this one. She's often depicted by a figure tenderly cradling a pentacle as though it's a child rather than a slab of gold.

Nurture is definitely part of who she is. But, though she offers care, that doesn't mean she does it softly. In fact, she grabs it with both hands. The Queen of Pentacles' relationship with the world is one of sensation. I like to think of her as an amalgamation of those countless fabulous fairy godparent characters in literature and film. They're anything from sixty-five to 105 (and there's literally no way to tell). Their homes are a living memory of the lives they've led, the places they've been, the people they've known. They are whirlwinds of jewel-toned silk dressing gowns, embroidered slippers, and bright lipsticks. They know what it is to live in the world and in the body, and offer that knowledge to anyone who needs it, with refreshments inappropriate to the hour, and the promise of more to come.

Like all of the Pentacles' court cards, the Queen's energy is focused on the material world: things that are real and tangible. This is the card of creature comforts. It lives by the William Morris principle of having nothing in your home that you do not know to be useful or believe to be beautiful. A Queen of Pentacles knows any object can be imbued with power and become a talisman, no matter how small or anonymous they seem. The act of perceiving something, of touching, seeing, and enjoying it, can change it – and it can change you. The Queen understands the power of the physical world upon the body and the mind: whether it's a perfectly brewed cup of tea, a scented candle, or a great work of art.

This character reminds you that you are allowed to have nice things, and you don't have to feel guilty about it. There's a happy medium between rampant consumerism and high asceticism, and this Queen symbolises the ability to find the balance. When this card appears, it invites you to consider whether you're striking that balance in your life. Are you starving yourself of comfort because you feel like you should? Or are you trying to fill a psychological, or even spiritual, gap with *things*? Are you allowing yourself to touch, and to be touched, in a healthy way?

I don't know that many people actually get to experience fairy godparents in their real lives. But surely it's telling that, so often, they appear in our stories. They are the mentors we all not-so-secretly wanted for our younger selves; the people we want to have known so that we can tell stories about them when we grow old. The Queen might be a rare spirit in her most distilled form, but she does exist, to some extent, in all of us: in our collective imaginations, and in those moments when we let ourselves be a little decadent, when we really treat ourselves, as an act of care. Ask yourself, who in your life offers that Queen of Pentacles energy to you? And to whom might you offer it?

QUESTIONS TO ASK WHEN YOU SEE THIS CARD: **Are you looking for nurture? What do you need from the world? Are there physical things or rituals that might ground you? Are you letting yourself appreciate material comforts?**

KING OF PENTACLES

SECURITY, WEALTH, RESPONSIBILITY, SUCCESS, MATERIAL
ATTAINMENT, GENEROSITY, HOARDING, AVARICE

Both the light and the shadow sides of the King of Pentacles
are very obvious in the way it's depicted in most decks. This
is a monarch with a *lot* of stuff. The King's throne is ornate,
grown over with vines and fruits. The outfit is the epitome of
maximalism – tell the tailor to make it plusher! More pleats,
more patterns, brighter colours! More! Often, this card shows
a figure sitting on a high mountain, uncut gems and coins at
their feet, wearing a crown of gold and flowers.

This can be aspirational or problematic. The King's palace
is a wonder trove, a cavern containing the wealth of the world,

sparkling and fabulous. The horned beasts carved into their throne are the riches of the land: herds of healthy bullocks and fattening ewes. But they could also be interpreted as sitting on a treasure cache, jealous as a slumbering dragon, or languishing with their fortune like Miss Havisham in *Great Expectations*. And the horned faces on the throne... well, let's just say there's someone with similar features in the Major Arcana, and it definitely isn't a friendly farm animal.

This King represents a time of plenty, or a successful person: one whose work and attitude has borne fruit. It speaks to material attainment: property, good health, racehorses, investments (maybe not cryptocurrency just yet – that feels like a Swords game). The quantity required for success isn't specified: you don't have to own three houses and a private jet to be a King of Pentacles. You just have to be comfortable. If you are, enjoy it. Take a moment to feel proud of whatever it is that you've built for yourself, and for those around you. This card, like all of the Kings, invites you to share what you know and have with the wider world. It asks: what, for you, is plenty? What is enough?

And what, do you think, might be more than enough? The King of Pentacles connotes wealth and security, but it can also speak to getting trapped by the desire for status and material possessions. We live in a society which believes that more is always better, and furthermore, that more is always possible. This King can act as a gentle reminder that there's no rule saying you have to keep playing the game forever. You don't always have to be striving for the next pay rise, the next promotion, the bigger house, and the fancier clothes. You particularly don't have to do that when the pursuit of success comes at the cost of your happiness and wellbeing.

There's a line in *Beowulf* about a dead ruler's burial hoard, which I think perfectly captures the gift and the challenge of the King of Pentacles: 'Gold on greot, þær hit nu gen lifað / eldum swa unnyt swa hit æror wæs,' – 'Gold in the earth, where it lies even now, as useless to men as it ever was.' Gold isn't totally useless, but that ancient poet knew its value is primarily social. By trading it and sharing it, you can build things: you can ensure your own security, and you can, perhaps, change lives for the better. In and of itself, though, it's just a shiny mineral. If you'd like to sit alone amassing your riches, counting them, guarding them (or, indeed, being buried with them), no one will stop you. But they might question whether you've understood the true meaning of wealth.

QUESTIONS TO ASK WHEN YOU SEE THIS CARD: Are you in a place of security right now? If not, what do you need to get there? Do you have enough, or do you have too much? Could you share your wealth with others? What does 'plenty' look like for you?

CHAPTER 6

The Wands

The metaphor of the Wands varies between different decks – they're also referred to as Rods or Batons – but, in most designs, the key visual theme is: big sticks. The sticks are used as building materials, as magic wands, and walking canes. Sometimes people are using the sticks to hit one another, and sometimes the sticks are just being carted around in massive bundles. The varied uses to which they are being put are good aide-memoires for each card's meanings. But there is one unchanging quality which speaks to the theme of the suit: the sticks are all flammable objects.

The Wands are the cards of fire, and it appears in all of its many forms in this suit: from a first spark that kindles something new, to a merry blaze that warms the heart, to a raging inferno, to a smoking ruin. Sometimes the fire of the Wands is benevolent and encouraging: it's the combustion engine that keeps things running smoothly, or the candle that lights the way. Sometimes it's out of control, a dangerous force of nature that can damage and hurt the people who get too close to it. And sometimes the difference between those things can be very small – just a matter of a change in the wind.

When dealing with the Wands, it's worth remembering that of the four elements that govern the suits of the tarot, fire is the only one that, on a scientific level, isn't actually elemental. It doesn't fit the definitions of solid, liquid, or gas like the others do. Fire isn't a substance; it's a reaction. It's what happens when you apply heat to fuel: an act of transformation, a special effect of energy shifting its state. This suit is the most changeable of the four, because its very essence is change. It doesn't have any specific corporeal associations, instead representing the spirit: the animating force of life and the constant transfer of energy.

The Wands speak to what we do, where we choose to channel our energy, and how the ebb and flow of that energy affects us physically and emotionally. It's about the transformative power which lives within us all. And, as you might expect, the journey through the suit is a dramatic one: there are remarkable highs and bone-weary lows. There are moments that feel great, and moments that are very uncomfortable indeed. In the Wands, you'll encounter talent, originality, charisma, adventure, sex, perseverance, and parties! But you'll also find conflict, fatigue, burnout, defeatism, delays, and deeply obnoxious people.

If you're doing a reading in which a lot of Wands turn up, it can be an opportunity to think about energy levels. There are times in our lives when we are full of high spirits, and times when we're running on empty, allowing our lanterns to dwindle down to almost nothing. These hot rods invite you to check in on how you're doing: are you burning brightly? Or do you need to refuel? You may also find that the capricious nature of this suit means that you flicker between different interpretations of the cards, seeing their shadow and light sides – their promises and pitfalls – in constant interplay.

More than anything, remember that with their elemental association to fire, the Wands represent power. Being able to tame and use fire has long been seen as what sets humans apart from the rest of the animal kingdom. It is the original act of creativity; the divine insight, stolen from the gods. Fire is what makes us what we are. Fire represents possibility. Fire is magnificent. And it is absolutely not to be played with.

ACE OF WANDS

In most decks, this is very much a 'say what you see' card. And what you'll see is a hand holding a wand. Not all wands are magic, but this one certainly is. It represents energetic potential: it's an unlit match, a firework ready to be set off.

On its most literal level, the Ace of Wands speaks to extraordinary possibilities: to willpower and talent and originality. It asks what kind of raw power burns at your core: what drives you, and where might it lead you if it were unleashed? It's an invitation to think about how you want to channel your energy and your passion. The wand isn't the source of the energy; it's a way of focusing it all in one direction – because *that* is how you get things done. When it appears, the Ace asks what you want to do and what you want to be. It invites you to realise your potential.

Like all of the Aces this card is usually a positive presence in a reading, but it still has a shadow side: speaking to moments when you lack energetic power and feel tired, or blocked, or stuck. Sometimes, this wand feels less like a conduit, and more like a spanner in the works: those situations when you know what you want to do but you just can't get yourself off the ground, or when people or circumstances delay or hold you back. The Ace holds within it the full potential of the suit: both its explosive highs and its exhausted lows. At the risk of leaning too heavily into the phallic overtones of the card's imagery, it's worth remembering that the opposite of potency is impotence. Sometimes the Ace of Wands invites you to brandish your power in the world – and sometimes, it allows you to acknowledge that, much as you might wish otherwise, it just isn't happening for you right now.

In either scenario, this card speaks to one of the tarot's all-time favourite topics: change. The Ace of Wands sits at the threshold of the new and the unknown, beckoning you to step through. It can be a spark, a 'sliding doors' moment, or a crisis. The crucial detail here is agency. There are plenty of moments in the tarot where change is something inevitable that must be accepted or adjusted to. That is absolutely not the energy of the Ace of Wands. The Ace of Wands isn't something that happens to you: it's you happening to something. And you do. You happen to the world every day. You can be a loose cannon, a serendipity engine, or an agent of chaos. Just by existing, you create change. The Ace of Wands is a reminder of the power that is vested in the simple and unavoidable act of *being*.

This card says that we all hold power in our hands, one way or another. And it prompts a primal instinct for what to do with it. Give a toddler a stick and, without any need for instruction, they'll point it at the sky, at the ground, at the people around them (often with appropriate sound effects). The Ace of Wands says: grab the magic wand. Wave the wand. Make something happen. You know you want to.

QUESTIONS TO ASK WHEN YOU SEE THIS CARD: Are you ready to change things? What inspires your greatest passions? Where do you want to focus your energy? Do you feel frustrated or held back? What's blocking you from taking action?

TWO OF WANDS

After the raw potential of the Ace, the Two of Wands is, on its simplest level, a card of getting started on something. It means the engine is turning over, the energy is building, and progress is being made. It's the feeling of putting one foot in front of the other, of finding your rhythm and moving with it. There aren't any pyrotechnics just yet – this is a smouldering fire, rather than a raging inferno – but the spark has found kindling and it is beginning to take hold. It's a wonderful feeling, isn't it, to know that you've got enough fuel to keep on feeding that flame? When this card turns up, it says that your metaphorical train has left the metaphorical station (toot toot!) and now you're on your way.

But, wait, what's this up ahead? Is that a fork in the tracks? I do believe it is. The Two of Wands is all about walking the path, but it doesn't make any promises about that path being a straight one. In fact, if it promises anything, it promises surprises. After all, this suit is the opposite of practical. It's constantly leaping around, ravenous and capricious and unpredictable. The Two of Wands is all about being faced with multiple paths, objectives, or possibilities. Quite often, when it appears in a reading, it invites a querent to consider a dilemma or a decision that they need to make: one that pertains to a significant goal in their life, or a personal quest. It speaks powerfully to the experience of finding yourself being drawn in two (or more) directions.

This is an age-old dilemma. For me, this card recalls the moment in Sylvia Plath's novel *The Bell Jar* in which the narrator sees her life 'branching out before me like the green fig tree in the story. From the tip of each branch, like a fat purple fig, a wonderful future beckoned and winked.' She could be a poet, a professor, a housewife, an Olympic athlete, or a thousand other things, but she hesitates to decide because 'choosing one meant losing all the rest.' She cuts to the heart of the difficulty of making choices: once you've done it, you have to live with the dream of what might have been as well as what is. You have to live with the knowledge that things might have been different if you'd chosen something else.

Sometimes, the fear of regretting a choice leads people to put off making decisions, preferring to cling to multiple unrealised potentials rather than forge forward in one direction that might or might not work out. The Two of Wands says that's no way to live. It asks you to stop worrying about making the perfect choice (if there even is such a thing). It's a reminder that, when you come to a fork in the road, you need to choose a direction to make progress – even when it's hard, even when it feels like doing so means snuffing out other opportunities. And there's a gift nestled in that too: because every single choice creates new possibilities. The tree of life branches out, and then it branches again, and again. So stop hesitating, and embrace the chance to choose your own adventure.

QUESTIONS TO ASK WHEN YOU SEE THIS CARD: What decisions are you facing right now? Do you feel paralysed by the possibilities? Are you trying to second-guess yourself? What does your gut tell you to do? What's the worst that could happen?

THREE OF WANDS

It's nice to have a goal in mind, isn't it? Half of the problem of getting something done is deciding what it is that you want to do in the first place (see: the Two of Wands). So, if you've managed to come up with a clear objective for yourself, well done! The other half of the problem is working out exactly how you're going to get from where you are to where you want to be... and that's what this card is all about.

The Three of Wands is the card of strategising. The Rider Waite Smith deck depicts it as a figure holding three wands, but the way I like to think of this card is to imagine that those aren't just sticks – they're planks. Specifically, they are planks that are going to be used to build a bridge. If you are on one side of a river and need to get to the other side, a bridge is probably your best option for a safe crossing. But you can't just imagine a bridge and float across. You have to build it. And to do that, you need to have all of the necessary materials; you need to know how everything will fit together in such a way that your construction will be sturdy and you will not suddenly find yourself soaking wet and freezing cold. In short, you need a good, solid plan.

So, when this card appears, it's a chance to examine whether or not such a plan exists. The Three of Wands can be a very pleasant card in a reading, cheerleading a querent who's working out what they need to do in order to achieve their goal. It can also prompt conversations about hopes and fears: does the querent feel confident in their planning? Are they worried that they might have missed something? The tarot can't offer much reassurance on this front (asserting that it's good to have a plan is one thing; having the expertise to be able to assess proposals is quite another), but it can be calming and helpful to at least acknowledge those anxieties out loud.

The other thing that this card sometimes flushes out is the total and utter absence of a plan. This is a familiar feeling for most people: those times when you know what you want to achieve but you have absolutely no idea how you're supposed to do it. It can be a very overwhelming situation in which to find oneself. And when that happens it can lead to deciding that the goal is just far too hard – impossible, actually – and throwing in the towel. The flip side of planning is giving up and, in its shadow side, the Three of Wands is very much the home of defeatism.

More than anything, then, this card should act as a reminder that it's good to try. We're increasingly told that children should be praised for their efforts, rather than their achievements, but I reckon the same is true of all people, no matter their age. Planning facilitates action and so, in speaking to one, the Three of Wands also encourages the other. It loves a plan, sure, but it loves a trier even more.

QUESTIONS TO ASK WHEN YOU SEE THIS CARD: Do you have a plan for how to achieve your goals? Are you being realistic about the amount of effort needed? Are you ready to give it a go and put your intentions into action? Or are you feeling like it's pointless to even try?

FOUR OF WANDS

CELEBRATION, REVELRY, JOY, COMMUNITY, GATHERINGS,
GRATITUDE, TOGETHERNESS

The Fours of the tarot are resting places in each of the suits. They offer a moment to pause and reflect on where you are and how your journey is going, with the tone of the moment reflecting the energy of the suit. And here, in the high-octane Wands, the flavour of that pause isn't quiet or contemplative. The flavour is PARTY.

This is a card that tells you to send out invitations to your nearest and dearest, find your sparkliest outfit, put up the gazebo, and prepare for revelry. If it were a hat, it'd be a party hat. If it were a biscuit, it'd be a Party Ring. If it were a playlist, it'd be filled with absolute bangers. I think you get the picture. In fact, you'd probably get the picture as soon as you saw this card, which – you guessed it – is usually an illustration of a party. The Four of Wands is a wholesome affair, though, rather than a rager. It reminds me of attending a flower-strewn dinner with seven near strangers, at which I had such a wonderful time that I didn't leave until 6am, after we had watched the sun rise from the host's roof with a fried egg and a glass of 'breakfast wine' each. It's the sort of party where you feel at home, laugh all night, and then wake up filled with the joy of being alive, rather than wishing you were dead.

Now, while it's all well and good for the tarot to tell you that it's time for a party, it doesn't tell you why. That's the first question that you get to ask your querent, or yourself: what's the occasion? Maybe it's a birthday, a marriage, a new home, an achievement, or just a chance to reconnect with beloved people. Regardless of the answer, the tarot gives you a seal of approval for your plans.

The second question is a little more introspective. It's about how you relate to acts of celebration. Some people feel completely comfortable asking friends, families, lovers, and strangers to show up for them – and others feel terrified by the thought of asking, let alone expecting it. Some people instinctively know how to celebrate themselves and some people really, really don't. Some people are natural party animals, others are whatever the opposite of that is (party... stones?). And some people have legendary talents for making events go off with a bang, which are occasionally exploited by those around them for hen weekends. So, where do you sit on that spectrum? Do you know how to bring the party? Do you know how to recognise when a party – however grand or intimate, literal or metaphorical – is called for? Do you feel deserving of parties? Do you want to have one now?

The answers to the questions above don't *have* to be yes, but the Four of Wands strongly implies that they should be. It's a reminder that it's not just alright to ask others to join you in celebrating your successes and achievements: it's healthy. It's an acknowledgement that knowing how to pull off a party is a skill, and one that merits appreciation. And it's telling you that, if you feel a celebration brewing, other people are probably more than ready to join you for it.

QUESTIONS TO ASK WHEN YOU SEE THIS CARD: Is there something that deserves to be celebrated in your life right now? Are you planning to mark the occasion? How do you want to celebrate? Do you feel comfortable asking people to show up for you?

FIVE OF WANDS

CONFLICT, IN-FIGHTING, FRUSTRATIONS, INCONVENIENCES,
LISTENING, OPEN-MINDEDNESS

This card, as is very obvious in its depictions in most decks, is a card of conflict and frustration: it's often illustrated by a group of people hitting one another with sticks in a not particularly convivial, but also not overly threatening, manner. This isn't a fight to the death, and it certainly isn't a war. It's arguments and quibbles and niggling annoyances. It's the slow grind of nagging tension, small disappointments, and best-laid plans going awry.

I find that the Five of Wands tends to refer to two different flavours of frustration, and that the way the card should be interpreted depends on which it is. The first is things just going wrong: precipitation on the day of your nuptials, being delayed by slow-moving vehicles, having too many pieces of one sort of cutlery when you need quite another. (Yes, it's *that* song.) And the second, which requires a little more care, is when the frustration comes from other people. It speaks to times when everyone wants to be heard and nobody is being listened to. Maybe you're trying to get something done, and no one will agree on how that ought to be achieved. Maybe people are poking holes in a perfectly good plan, and you're ready to tear your hair out at their inability to understand what you're trying to say, or just to trust you.

Or maybe you're trying to force a square peg into a round hole. Are those dissenting voices just irritating flies buzzing in your ears, or do they have something useful to say? We all know how nice it is to be right, and how easy it can be to filter out conflicting information (I believe they call this 'confirmation bias'). After a while, it's hard to remember that there was ever another option. The Five of Wands sometimes appears to remind you that, if you want to effect change, if you really want to be a transformative force, you can't just dismiss other ideas and approaches, or pretend they don't exist. You need to engage with them. Sometimes, you even need to be able to acknowledge that you've made a mistake (I know!), and change your approach.

This isn't to say that you're wrong, and it's not a principle to be applied to fundamental moral or ethical values. But the gift of the Five of Wands is the knowledge that, if you don't permit yourself to be challenged, you deny yourself the opportunity to grow – whether that's by strengthening your position, or re-evaluating it. Diversity of thought can be a catalyst for change: some of the most brilliant and original acts of creativity and ingenuity come from allowing people who wouldn't normally interact to spark off one another. Clashes of opinion aren't always enjoyable, but they can be important. In fact, they can be generative. This card asks, what might you do with that friction? Could it be useful to you?

The other gift of this card is for those less lofty moments of frustration, when you aren't having your mind and perspectives expanded . . . you've just stubbed your toe, spilled tea all over yourself, are wrestling with a jammed printer, and really need to vent. Some people might ask you: is this ironic? NO is what the Five of Wands would answer. No, this is NOT irony. This is just VERY ANNOYING INDEED.

QUESTIONS TO ASK WHEN YOU SEE THIS CARD: Where are you experiencing conflict in your life? What's at the heart of it? Are you sure you're in the right? Could you learn from someone else? Do you just need to vent? (Go for it.)

SIX OF WANDS

VICTORY, ACHIEVEMENT, SELF-DEVELOPMENT, CONFIDENCE, PRIDE, MOMENTUM, AMBITION, ONWARDS

Somewhat oddly, the Wands is the suit in the tarot where you get the most martial imagery. You might expect fighting to be the preserve of the Swords, but you would be wrong: with the Swords, you are mostly either being threatened or you are dead. The in-between states, the being-hit-with-something experiences, largely belong to the Wands. After all, a wooden staff is more likely to leave a bruise than a mortal wound. It's a training weapon, an opportunity to learn from mistakes, rather than be ended by them.

With that in mind, say hello to the Six of Wands: the card of the experienced warrior. In the Rider Waite Smith, it's depicted by a figure crowned in laurels riding a horse, with a backdrop of flags raised for victory. It's a parade! A parade for winners! A victory parade! It's a sight for sore eyes and a balm for bruised bodies. This card is all about the moments when things are going your way. It's an acknowledgement that effort – and, yes, sometimes conflict – can pay off. It's the feeling of satisfaction that comes from a win, from knowing you acquitted yourself as well as you could have hoped. It's pride in yourself and what you've been able to do.

The Sixes of the tarot ask what you've learned, and what you can do with your lessons – and this one is no exception. This isn't the naive and hopeful energy of someone who has just set out on their journey. The Six is a seasoned traveller, one who's forded rivers, weathered storms, met friends and foes along the way. Their cloak has been patched a few times, there's dirt under their fingernails, and they've got some excellent stories to tell around the campfire.

When it appears, it asks you to glance backwards and take stock of your experiences. What are the things that have made you who you are? How have you been built and shaped by the world? How do you measure your success and your failures? It recalls a passage in Virginia Woolf's *The Waves*, where one of the six narrators describes the ways in which they have each carved themselves from their raw potential: 'We were all different. The wax – the virginal wax that coats the spine melted in different patches for each of us.' The Six of Wands reminds us that living changes us; it leaves an impression on us. We develop patinas, unique sets of markings – scars, badges of honour, and mementoes – that we should treasure, because they're all part of how we tell our stories.

What the Six of Wands definitely isn't is the end of your journey. It's a moment to recognise how far you've come, and to think about where you still want to go. So what's next? Well, that part remains to be seen. Probably a few more battles and a few more scars, if we're honest, but hopefully some more triumphs too. More work, more effort, more to do, and more to think about. More to discover, more to become. The Six of Wands reminds you that you've got this. You're strong. Your people are around you and your noble steed is beneath you (probably not a real horse, but who knows). So raise your flag, kick your heels, and continue. ONWARDS!

QUESTIONS TO ASK WHEN YOU SEE THIS CARD: What have you achieved? What do you feel proud of having done? What motivates you? What have you learnt along the way, and how will that serve you as you continue? Are you ready to move forward? Are you excited?

SEVEN OF WANDS

CONVICTION, BELIEF, PERSEVERANCE, STUBBORNNESS, FAITH,
PRINCIPLES, BETRAYAL OF PRINCIPLES

I have long felt that the saying, 'Is that the hill you're going to die on?' is an unfairly maligned one. The implication is always that, by sticking to whatever it is you're sticking to, you are being foolishly stubborn and will meet a bad end. Granted, there are probably some hills which aren't worth the effort... but what about the ones that are? What about the times when you get to say, yes, actually. Yes, this is that hill.

The Seven of Wands is all about the battle that you have picked, and the hill that you are prepared to defend at all costs. It's a card of stubbornness, certainly, but in the best possible way. It's about persevering and holding true to your beliefs. Earlier in this suit (the Five), we met a card that's all about the moments when being challenged can be healthy, because it opens us up to change and growth. The Seven might look similar on the surface, but it has a different perspective. The Seven tells you to keep on fighting the good fight. It tells you that there is something valuable – extraordinary even – in being able to hold to your convictions, especially when you're faced with pressure to back down. It can and should remind you of the moments when one person's refusal to betray their principles has made the world a better place.

When I see this card, I'm also reminded of the times in my life when I haven't quite managed to do that. We all capitulate once in a while, bowing to the so-called wisdom of the group, even when it feels quite unwise. We do things that we don't feel comfortable with because it's expected of us, because it's 'normal'. I think mainly of moments early in my career when I didn't say or do what I knew was right, because it was clear that I'd risk losing my job if I did. I look back at my younger self and understand why she made the safe choice. But I've also realised that doing so always took something out of me – and sometimes it took too much. As I've grown older, I've tried to channel the Seven of Wands more: to know what my boundaries are, and to hold fast to them no matter what.

The words 'no matter what' are where the shadow lies in this card. When you make a decision to go to bat for something and put all of your energy into it, you can triumph. You can be vindicated by being on the right side of history, or even just by the immediate consequences. But you can also, metaphorically, die on the hill. So you need to be prepared. You need to be ready to go full last-ride-of-the-Rohirrim down that hill. (For those who aren't familiar with *Lord of the Rings*, that means charging towards an almost unwinnable fight, screaming 'RIDE TO

RUIN AND THE WORLD'S ENDING!' i.e. a major commitment and also quite a look.)

So, is this the hill you're going to die on? Time will tell. The Seven only asks you to make sure that you've picked your battleground in service of doing what you believe is right.

QUESTIONS TO ASK WHEN YOU SEE THIS CARD: What are the principles you hold that you would never compromise? When have you felt like you've capitulated to pressure? Is there something you feel like you're being asked to back down on? Can you persevere?

EIGHT OF WANDS

DECISIVE ACTION, MOMENTUM, RAPID TRANSFORMATION, SELF-
EMPOWERMENT, SELF-BELIEF, BLOCKING, HOLDING YOURSELF BACK

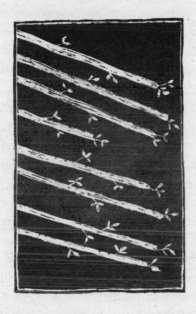

The Eight of Wands is a card that trips a lot of people up when they first start reading the tarot. It's certainly one that we both struggled with and, unusually, even the iconography of the card isn't hugely helpful in most decks. It's just a picture of a lot of sticks? The Eights of the tarot are usually about transitions and transformations, but the Wands are all about raw energy – fire – which is already in a constant state of flux. How can transformative power itself be transformed? It's a good question and, fortunately, we have the answer.

For us, the most perfect illustration of this card isn't what's drawn on it. It's a line from the musical masterpiece *Tight Pants / Body Rolls* by Leslie Hall: a song that has long had a special place in our hearts. It's the one Fiona and I put on and dance ('dance') to when we're feeling giddy, when the only way to let out some wild Wands-y energy is to perform the move formally known as the high kick. Its lyrics describe an unusual version of the hero's journey: a woman, wandering through a forest, meets a little creature wearing magical leggings. She gazes upon him in awe, and then implores him to make a pair of those leggings for her too. Because, oh, how her life would be changed by a pair of those tight pants! Oh, the marvellous things she could do while wearing them! The elf agrees to help her and gets to work. But then, at the final moment, just as he finishes the last stitch, she looks down . . . and experiences a dazzling revelation about herself: 'I was already wearing tight pants. I just did not ACTIVATE them.'

This is the message of the Eight of Cups. This card tells you that you are *already wearing* your magical leggings. You have everything you need: the power to enact change is within you. Stop looking beyond yourself, stop waiting for some external force to sweep you up. Stop telling yourself that you'll do this thing or start that journey once X, Y, or Z is in place, or once someone else gives you the permission or the push to do it. You don't need to do any more charging up or any more preparation. You need to activate your own power – and the moment to do it is right now. The Eight of Cups is both a green light for action, and a call to trust in yourself to be able to pull something off. It's a pep talk; a battle cry. It's RELEASE THE HOUNDS (you are the hounds).

When this card appears, it conjures the sense of things moving and falling into place fast. It's a reminder to strike while the iron is hot, to let momentum do what it does best: carry you forwards. And it's a chance to reflect on whether or not you're holding yourself back. It says stop resisting, stop pretending this is a slow burn when it isn't. It's a bonfire. The music is loud and it's riotous, it's possibly more than 180bpm, and it's calling to you. So put on your very best, very tightest, pants, and dance.

QUESTIONS TO ASK WHEN YOU SEE THIS CARD: Is there something you're putting off? Are you waiting for the perfect moment to act? Why aren't you acting now? What more do you need to do this thing? What's blocking you from acting? What colour are your tight pants?

NINE OF WANDS

This is a card about having a lot of wands. By 'wands' the tarot means: things to do. And by 'a lot' it means: far too many. It can be too many commitments, too many demands on your time, too much on your mind, or just too many places to channel your energy. Sometimes, in the moment, it doesn't feel like it's too much: you can convince yourself that it's absolutely manageable, or perhaps even feel a little proud of how much you can carry. But this card is a reminder (if not exactly a forewarning) that if you don't leave space for those unexpected extra demands on your time and energy, you'll struggle when they inevitably land in your lap. You know that saying about the straw that breaks the camel's back? Well, this is the tarot's polite way of saying 'no more straw for you, pal'.

On a practical level, the Nine of Wands invites you to take inventory of everything you're carrying and consider if it's all necessary. What would happen if you didn't do it? Would everything collapse, or would it actually be totally fine? This card is an advocate for setting boundaries: knowing what's within your limits and what's going to push you over the edge. As an extraordinary teacher once asked me after I'd had an hour-long weep in her office: are you trying to always shine at 100 watts, when perhaps 60 watts would do? (I was.)

The Nine of Wands also speaks to the importance of asking for help when you need it, whether that's in the form of practical action, emotional support, or something more. This card is a good representation of the inner life of someone walking into their first counselling session – which, incidentally, is exactly what I did after the 100-watt lightbulb conversation. Sometimes, the biggest barrier to lightening your load is not trusting anyone else to carry it quite as well as you do. Sometimes it's not believing that anyone would want to help you shoulder your burden. This Nine can be a reminder that neither of those things are true.

It is, of course, possible for this card to appear in a spread as something you need more of in your life. This is a delicate space, but it's definitely worth asking the question of a querent. Do they feel guilty that they aren't able to provide more help and support to others – even when they know that it's not physically possible? Once in a while, you might even find that this card *does* prompt someone to acknowledge that maybe they aren't pulling their weight. Perhaps they're letting their partner take on the lion's share of domestic labour, or letting colleagues pick up slack at work. The tarot doesn't judge anyone, but it creates opportunities for people to be honest with themselves and others, and to ask themselves why they're behaving that way.

As with all of the Nines in the tarot, this card exists in dialogue with the one that follows it: it's a sneak preview, a teaser of what's to come if you continue in this direction. You're on a fast train – next stop, the Ten of Wands – and, trust me, that isn't where you want to end up. This is your chance to course-correct. Take it.

QUESTIONS TO ASK WHEN YOU SEE THIS CARD: Are you doing too much? Can you put something down? No, really, can you? Are you feeling guilty or like you aren't pulling your weight? Is that legitimate or not? What can you do to change it?

TEN OF WANDS

The good thing about this card is that it's one which rarely requires a huge amount of explanation. Most of the time, when this is turned over, the querent immediately says something along the lines of, 'Oh, yes, I know what this is. I FEEL THIS.' And the bad thing about it is that this is not a pleasant way to feel. Not at all.

The Ten of Wands represents what happens when you've had too much on your plate, and are no longer able to deal with it. It is the card of being incredibly exhausted. It is the broken camel. It's the card of burnout. You have tried to carry too many wands. They were very heavy, you're very tired, and you have reached the point where you can't do it any more and you need to find a way to let go. In fact, you are going to let go, whether you like it or not. Everyone's energy runs out at some point, and usually at the worst possible moment. The Ten of Wands speaks to the danger of going past the point where you can manage a controlled descent, one that preserves the things that matter most. It says that you are either about to fall dramatically out of the sky or, sometimes, that you have already reached that point, and are now a pile of blazing wreckage. Or a husk.

Hindsight is a wonderful thing and, when this card appears, many of the lessons and questions of the Nine of Wands suddenly feel like things you *really* should have paid attention to earlier. It's something of an 'I told you so' about what happens when we don't set boundaries and ask for help when we need it. But if it's already too late, and you didn't take the emergency action, where does that leave you? What can you do now? How can you fix it? You've got far too much on to have burnout, so what's the solution? There must be something you can do to fix it, right? Right?!

I hope you can see what I'm getting at here. The Ten of Wands speaks to a quite recognisable, self-destructive behaviour: when you're so worn out that you aren't actually able to do anything useful, but you still won't accept it. Your brain is running on a metaphorical hamster wheel: you're expending lots of energy, but going absolutely nowhere. There's more than a touch of masochism to the Ten of Wands, and it very powerfully recalls the beguiling, ever-retreating horizon of ultimate productivity. It's easy to feel that if you just worked a little harder, did a little more, you might finally get there. This card is here to gently, but firmly, prise your fingers away from that tightly gripped fiction. You cannot push yourself any harder.

The only way to recover from burnout is to rest. You need a break and you need it right now, no matter how inconvenient the timing.

The challenges of this card are many and obvious. But what, you might be asking, is its gift? The best answer is that it's the same gift you get when you finally cease hitting your own head on a brick wall. It feels good to stop. *Please*, says the Ten of Wands, *please would you just put those sticks down*.

QUESTIONS TO ASK WHEN YOU SEE THIS CARD: Are you OK? What can you stop doing? How can you take a break? Do you feel like you have to be busy all the time? Why?

PAGE OF WANDS

ADVENTURE, DISCOVERY, WONDER, EXPLORATION, TRAVEL,
PERSONAL GROWTH, FLIGHTINESS, IMPRACTICALITY

The best way to understand the Page of Wands is to cast your
mind back to your childhood, to the young heroes and hero-
ines of nearly every book you ever read. You'll notice, if you
haven't before, that there is an extraordinary preponderance of
orphans in children's literature. And, while the Page of Wands
has nothing to do with bereavement, it has everything to do
with behaving like a plucky storybook orphan.

The key benefit of orphanhood, according to these books
anyway, is that you don't have anyone to tell you what to
do, so you get to do whatever you want. You're alone in the

world, constrained by neither the daily chores and rituals and 'because I said so' of protective parents (snooze), nor the social, professional, and domestic obligations of adulthood (boring!). Your sense of danger is dull at best, and you slip through the cracks because you are literally a small child. You can stow away on a pirate ship, join the circus, be raised by wolves, find a portal to another world, become an international spy, wizard, cosmonaut, or jewel thief, or just get really good at horse-riding. In short, you get to have ADVENTURES.

This trope is, obviously, an unrealistic depiction of what actually happens when children are separated from their care-givers. But it's deeply embedded in our cultural imagination because it's such a pure and uncomplicated vision of freedom: no ties, no one to whom you owe a courtesy call, no one else's rules or ideas of you shaping your identity. We all, on some level, want to be the Page of Wands: the wonder-child, the little adventurer who follows their whims and encounters some challenges and low-grade peril on the way to a satisfying con-clusion. This card is a reminder of that desire, a taste of that feeling, and an invitation to consider how (or if) adventure is being manifested in your life. It can be a breath of fresh air or a call of the wild: an interruption, a suggestion to try something new, to go somewhere else.

Mostly, this Page represents a new opportunity or perspec-tive for a querent. Sometimes it brings up very literal changes of scene – holidays weren't really a thing when the tarot was born, but these cards are nothing if not adaptable to the many marvellous inventions of the modern world. And sometimes the shift is in mindset: a chance discovery about oneself, or an escape from old patterns of thinking or assumptions that have held you back. Whether or not these revelations and new opportunities will turn out to be realistic or practical is a whole other debate – indeed, this Page is definitely the home of flights of fancy that sometimes need to be tempered with a dose of pragmatism. But isn't it refreshing to allow space in our lives for novelty, and for personal growth?

The court cards usually speak to people we know or aspects of ourselves, but they can also be understood as embodiments of particular feelings. For me, the Page of Wands recalls a line from a Keats poem that expresses the heart-lifting sensation of encountering something new and marvellous: 'Then I felt like some watcher of the skies / When a new planet swims into his ken.' This card reminds us that the world is out there, that it's huge and strange and full of unknowable possibilities. It's an invitation to wonder.

QUESTIONS TO ASK WHEN YOU SEE THIS CARD: **Where do you want to go? What do you want to explore? Do you give yourself permission for adventure? Do you indulge your fancies enough – or too much?**

KNIGHT OF WANDS

IMPULSIVITY, ACTION, CONVICTION, DETERMINATION,
SEDUCTION, UNPREDICTABILITY

There's a lot to be said about the Knight of Wands, but there's one thing that I need to get out of the way before we broach any of this card's subtleties (such as they are). I need to tell you that this is the horniest card in the tarot. The Knight of Wands is a ride in every sense of the word. It's perfectly possible – also quite entertaining – to read the tarot through the lens of the bedroom, but this is the card that most simply and straight-forwardly telegraphs sex. It is the card of intense physical chemistry, even (especially) when it's inexplicable. It's the card of someone being your own personal brand of catnip. It's the card of crushes and connections and pheromones. Sometimes, that's all you need to know and exactly how to interpret it.

Scratch beneath the surface, though, and you'll see that a libidinous interpretation of the Knight of Wands is just one way of understanding it – although it's a fairly good metaphor for the temperament and qualities that the card represents overall. The Knight of Wands is all about action: they're on a mission, charging ahead, obsessive and demanding and all-consuming. This Knight is electric. This Knight is a forest fire. This Knight, in the words of our lord and saviour, Lorde, is a liability. Knights of Wands are impulsive and unpredictable, a burning energy which can race right through you and set you alight before you even notice what's happening, or have a chance to think about the potential dangers.

And the thing is that sometimes that's exactly what you need. There are times for caution and careful risk analyses, and there are times when the only way to effect change is to just jump into something and hope for the best. The strategy of this Knight is to ask for forgiveness, not permission (in fact, they don't always bother with the forgiveness part). Not everyone enjoys chaos, but you can't argue that it's the perfect antidote to inertia. There are moments when you need to be this guy: to be fearless and take risks in pursuit of your dreams and your goals.

There are also times when you really, really don't need to be like that. I always feel that the Knights of the tarot have some of the most obvious dualities within them: their shadow sides loom large, and their challenges can be more significant than their gifts. It probably isn't too hard to see the cautionary tale in this one: the potential for solipsistic or even slightly dangerous behaviour. For me, this card recalls the sensation of mania: having too much energy skittering through your body, feeling as though the world is slow and plodding and you are a comet raging through it. It's a high that doesn't end well. Just like those moments of amazing physical chemistry, the blaze of glory is often followed by a rather less satisfying fall.

More than anything, the Knight of Wands asks whether you're in control of your actions. Things are happening – perhaps very fast, or very dramatically – and it takes a firm hand to ensure that they don't run away with you. So keep hold of the reins, and try your best to enjoy the ride.

QUESTIONS TO ASK WHEN YOU SEE THIS CARD. Who is the biggest agent of change in your life right now? Are you in control of the trajectory, or are you in danger? Are you just having a fabulous sexy time? (Who's the lucky person?)

QUEEN OF WANDS

CHARM, FREE-SPIRITEDNESS, ATTRACTIVENESS, BRILLIANCE,
RADIANCE, POPULARITY, SOCIAL DYNAMICS, CLIQUES

'Be the flame, not the moth' is a quote widely attributed to Giacomo Casanova – or, at least, it's a quote attributed to him by the 2005 film *Casanova*, starring Heath Ledger, which is good enough for me. Regardless of its historical origins, it is very definitely the motto of the Queen of Wands. This person is always the flame: charming, attractive, compelling, radiant. You know a Queen of Wands as soon as you meet one: you are drawn to them; you want to get to know them better; you want to be them. Queens of Wands are the brightest and most brilliant people in any room, summoning attention to themselves like bees to nectar.

At their best, a Queen of Wands is like Dolly Parton. Their sparkle is channeled into action: the greater the challenge, the higher they rise; the bigger the platform, the bigger the hair. They are defined by self-belief, by courage, and by ambition. They give their time, their energy, and their resources to the things that matter to them – and their convictions are so strong and so intoxicating that other people find themselves unable to resist going along with them, for better or for worse. This card represents that person about whom your parents would ask, 'If they told you to jump off a bridge, would you?' (You would, obviously.)

And that's the key to understanding its darker side. There's a reason we're warned not to play with fire – just because something looks beautiful, doesn't mean it can't hurt you. At their worst, this Queen is Regina George in *Mean Girls*. If you get too close, you might get burnt, and yet, somehow, still want more. If that shadow-self emerges, it's usually because a Queen of Wands has been trapped by their own glamour and reduced to that one popular aspect of themself. Deprived of the opportunity to be authentic and multi-faceted, or forced to perform the same tired role over and over again, they can become caustic.

More often than not, the Queens of the tarot are benevolent presences in the deck: invitations to give more freedom to certain parts of yourself, or to enjoy the company of people who embody those characteristics. So unless this card appeared in a particularly leading position in a spread, I'd always lean towards its more positive interpretations: relishing its vivacity, charm, and passion. But it shouldn't be forgotten that self-awareness is the greatest strength of all of the Queens – and this is probably the one who needs it the most. Sometimes the people who burn the brightest are the least aware of how their presence or absence can affect others.

I like to think of the Queen of Wands as a pillar of flame that casts a circle of light around itself. To be within that circle is to be seen, to be under the Queen's protection, bathed in the warmth of their regard. But it's also worth considering who sits outside that space (particularly if you recognise this Queen in yourself). It's easy for people to find themselves competing for attention and, if they don't get it, feeling invisible or unseen. A Queen of Wands chooses whom they invite to their side. The challenge lies in acknowledging that their choices can have consequences, and exercising care in making them.

QUESTIONS TO ASK WHEN YOU SEE THIS CARD: Who in your life is a shining beacon right now? Are you a beacon for others? What does it mean to be the centre of attention? Is it something you want, something you admire, or something you just witness?

KING OF WANDS

VISIONARY, GENIUS, CHARISMA, AGGRESSION,
DOMINANCE, HYPER-MASCULINITY

If you were to describe the King of Wands in a single word, that word would be 'visionary'. This character is all about bringing the raw energy and transformative power of the Wands to bear. This is the ultimate end point of the suit: the moment at which its fire and passion are harnessed, brought to heel, and put to work. The King is capable of incredible things: they're charismatic, inspiring, exciting, and able to bring others with them on the journey, to fire them up with the desire to put plans into action. And they know it. They have what we might refer to as Big Wand Energy.

With this King, when a querent is asked whether it reminds them of themselves or of someone they know, they usually say that it's the latter. There are very few people out there who will say, 'Hi, yes, that's me, the magnetic and inspirational leader.' Most would also instinctively know that, while the King of Wands can represent people who pull off the most amazing feats – turning around failing institutions, galvanising jaded teams, breaking new frontiers of innovation–it also bears more than a passing resemblance to some rather less aspirational public figures. The line between visionary genius and deluded megalomaniac can be very fine, and it's not wrong to approach it with caution. At full blaze, this character is a lot. When the tarot suggests that you might want to be more King of Wands, it always lets you choose to what degree.

It is also worth talking to querents about how they respond to the Kings of Wands already present in their lives. The energy of this card is hyper-masculine, although certainly not the exclusive preserve of men. It conjures a particular type of alpha-dominant behaviour which, while it can be very effective or even beguiling in the right circumstances, is often intimidating to interact with. Quite often, when the King of Wands appears, a querent is looking for advice on how to handle them. If you hold in your mind the governing element of the suit, you'll find a tool: a little piece of advice that isn't always easy to pull off but, in a strange and paradoxical way, makes perfect sense. This King is the ruler of fire – thus, fire is its weapon. And what do we fight fire with? That's right: more fire.

The truth is that the only thing a King of Wands respects is another King of Wands. Which means that if you need to take on a King of Wands and you haven't got your own to hand (a friend, a family member, a hired contractor), your best bet is to try to look like one. And how do you do that? Well, as someone who has worked in an industry with a fairly high quota of this personality type, I offer up a mantra that has served me well: TELL NO LIES, SHOW NO FEAR. Don't ever let them realise that they make you nervous – or even that you're impressed by them – because that will only stoke the blaze of their power. Stand your ground and hold your head high.

Got it? Well, look at you go. Maybe there's more King of Wands in you than you thought.

QUESTIONS TO ASK WHEN YOU SEE THIS CARD: Do you feel like you have the power to influence others? Do you have a vision that you want to see manifested? What will it take to achieve that? What is driving you? Are there charismatic people in your life who you struggle to handle?

CHAPTER 7

The Swords

I t is no accident that, of the four suits of the Minor Arcana, we've left the Swords until last. This is the suit in which the most difficult cards of the Minors make their home, and it's easier to get to know them – and to be able to see both their challenges and their gifts – if you're already broadly familiar with the pattern of the suits.

The Swords are aligned with the element of air: the invisible matter without which we cannot survive for more than a few moments. Invisible does not mean intangible, though. Air can be cool and calm, allowing you to fill your lungs and to exhale the things you don't need. And it can blow and buffet, knocking you to your knees, tearing up landscapes, and devastating lives. It's the element of both the life-giving reflex of breath and the destructive vortex of a hurricane. And it would be fair to say that most people, when asked what object best embodies the quality of air, probably wouldn't say 'big shiny sword'. To get to the bottom of the tarot's symbolism here, you need to also consider the aspect of the self to which it pertains.

When we're talking swords in the tarot, we are actually talking about the mind. This suit is all about the things that happen in our massively complicated, highly developed brains: our thoughts, our beliefs, our attitudes. The Swords are the home of both the positive and the negative sides of thinking. In this suit, you'll find lightbulb moments, clarity and problem-solving, the ability to learn and reason and make progress; wisdom lives here, along with debate. Also: sleeping, because the Swords know that a healthy mind is a rested mind. On the more difficult side, you'll find sorrow and heartache, anxiety and trauma, cruelty and coldness – patterns of thinking that entrap and damage you.

When you think of it like that, the metaphor of a sword begins to make a little more sense. Swords can be dangerous – get on the wrong end of one and it'll cut you to bloody ribbons. But in the right hands, and with the right training, it can cut through any knot. A skilled thinker is as impressive as an expert in sword-play: both display twists and turns of agility that can take your breath away with their rapid parries or quick flashes of insight. When people say that the pen is mightier than the sword, what they actually mean is that a strong mind can be more powerful and influential than a strong body. And perhaps, if the tarot was born of a more widely literate society, the pen might have been chosen to represent this aspect of the self rather than a blade.

Regardless of the rightness or wrongness of using a dangerous weapon as a metaphor for the human mind, the truth at this suit's core remains the same. The Swords speak both to our ability to leverage our thoughts to beneficial ends, and to our capacity to be wounded by them. There are images in this suit, in almost every deck you'll find, that are confronting: illustrations that depict suffering and pain. But there are also images that are uplifting, inspiring, and empowering. The contrasts between them render their truths all the more starkly.

The overarching lesson of the Swords is that the tool derives meaning from the way in which it is wielded. The fact that thoughts cannot be seen doesn't make them any less significant an influence in your life. But you *can* challenge patterns of thinking and, if you need to, you can change them.

ACE OF SWORDS

The Swords may be the suit of the mind, but the best way to understand their Ace is actually via a feeling – and it's usually a very good feeling indeed. It's the feeling you get when you've been stuck in a dull place for a while, shuffling through the same old bits of information and not really knowing what to do with them. And then, lo, out of nowhere: a breakthrough! Something occurs to you – maybe it's a small detail you finally notice, or maybe it's a fundamental shift in your perspective, but suddenly everything changes.

The Ace of Swords is, basically, the moment in a murder

mystery where the camera slowly zooms in on the detective's face and you watch their expression as they put together all of the clues and work out who did it. In other words, the patron saint of the Ace of Swords is Angela Lansbury as crime-novelist-turned-investigator Jessica Fletcher in *Murder, She Wrote*. It is the card of the lightbulb moment; the card of a flash of understanding; the card of having a spectacular realisation about something. At its purest and simplest, it represents an idea. It's about seeing the truth of a situation, and shattering previous assumptions. When it appears, it invites you to consider whether you've recently had a moment of revelation, or if you seek one. More importantly, it asks: what are you going to do with your new-found insight?

This is where things get a little more tricksy, and where the Ace reveals its double edge. In the tarot, that glorious eureka moment is usually depicted by a giant hand which breaks through a bank of clouds, wielding a sword. As an image it's... well, it's a little bit threatening. The thing about swords is that you tend to only need them when you're going into battle. So, are you? Is your new idea, your moment of realisation, about to lead you into conflict with others? And, if so, how will you conduct yourself in that engagement? The Swords, more so than any other suit, pertain to how you communicate with others: not just the content of what you say, but the delivery; the words you choose and the tone you use. There's a warning about being too sharp, too blunt, too aggressive in your interactions. You might have exactly the right idea, but if you don't find the right way to explain it, then a metaphorical lightbulb is probably all it will ever be.

The Ace of Swords offers up marvellous possibilities: every invention, every new and wonderful thing made in the world once began as an idea, an inkling about a way to do things a little bit differently. But taking a theory and making it into something real and solid usually requires securing the co-operation and support of others and, if you handle that badly, you'll scupper yourself before you even get started. Jessica Fletcher never solved a case by being combative and imperious – she was discerning, exacting, and focused, but always polite. Perhaps it's worth taking a leaf out of her book on this one.

QUESTIONS TO ASK WHEN YOU SEE THIS CARD: Are you facing a situation that could benefit from clear thinking or a fresh perspective? Do you have a new insight or angle or idea that you want to work on? Have you just realised something important? What will you do with that information? Do you know how to communicate it to others?

TWO OF SWORDS

DECISIONS, CONVICTION, AUTHORITY,
TRUSTING YOURSELF, STALEMATE, PARALYSIS

The main topic of conversation that this card prompts when it appears is decisions. Specifically, whether or not a querent is any good at making them. And, this being the Swords, we're talking about the intricate sort of decisions: the problem-solving ones, the ones which come with a full sheet of pros and cons, interdependencies, and cause-and-effect scenarios that need to be thought through and evaluated before you can come to a conclusion. The human brain isn't always great at those. You can run yourself ragged trying to second-guess outcomes, overthinking them so extravagantly that you can no longer see the wood for the trees.

Unsurprisingly, then, the Two of Swords might prompt you to think about a problem that you're facing, or have recently faced, one which feels complex and overwrought. Are you stuck staring at multiple solutions you could go with, unsure which one is right?

What I've always liked about this card is that, in an oblique way, it offers up a suggestion about how to proceed. To me, it calls to mind those people who seem to be weirdly good at making decisions: the kind of people who others turn to – in a tricky meeting at work, or trapped in a foreign airport at midnight when it turns out the trains aren't running any more, or at the lowest point of a disaster movie – and ask, 'What are we going to do now?' They get asked that because, somehow, you know that they're going to have an answer. You can't put your finger on what exactly it is about them that gives them their ability to be decisive, to make a call, and to stick to it with conviction, but it's a very reassuring trait, and one out of which some people successfully forge whole careers.

Maybe you're one of those people already (congratulations if so!). But maybe you're not. And if you're not, the Two of Swords would like to whisper the secret of becoming one to you. The secret is that those people actually don't know for sure. Not really. They are just as unable to predict the outcome of their decisions as you are – they aren't psychics. At best, they might know more about the subject than the other people in the room, or have more practice at rapidly assimilating and distilling all the information they're given. But their greatest gift is in knowing there's always more than one right answer, and that the wrongest thing you can do is to sit on the fence, paralysed by indecision. Two of Swords people trust themselves to do the best they can with the information that's in front of them. If they think a crucial data point is missing, they'll ask for it and, if it can't be found, they'll extrapolate and make an educated guess. This kind of decisiveness might look like a magical power, but it's not. It's a skill, and it's one that you're capable of strengthening if you wish.

More than anything, the Two of Swords knows that sometimes you just have to make a decision in order to move forwards. Nobody is expecting you to be right all of the time. But if you can take a step with confidence and conviction, you're far more likely to get to wherever it is you want to go. Maybe you already knew that. If not – well, now you do.

QUESTIONS TO ASK WHEN YOU SEE THIS CARD: **Are you struggling with a decision? Are you feeling overwhelmed by options? Do you find it easy to cut through and make a call? Do you trust yourself to choose a path? Could you try to?**

THREE OF SWORDS

HEARTACHE, SORROW, PAIN, HURT, TRAUMA, RELEASING PAIN,
GROWTH, INTEGRATION, HEALING

Let's just get this out of the way: this isn't the best card in the
tarot. You'll have probably already guessed that, what with
the picture of the heart being pierced by three swords. It's a
very powerful depiction of pain: of what it feels to be hurting
or heartbroken. Heartache comes in many forms, and it has
many causes, some of which are quite obvious (the end of a
relationship) and others that are harder to pin down: events or
experiences that move you deeply, or cut you to the very core.

If that's something that's going on in your life – well, you
won't need the tarot to tell you so. This card isn't about the

fact of pain; it's about what you do with it. It's about how you handle a wound to the heart: whether it breaks you, or whether you can find a way to allow it to bring you to a greater understanding of yourself, to allow you to change and grow. It's about how you can use your mind to help make sense of your feelings: to help you understand what those experiences mean to you and what you want to make of them. I like to think of its appearance in a reading as an invitation to confront pain and discomfort, and explore your response to it. If you're going through something that hurts, how are you handling it? Is it reopening a badly healed wound and hurting all the more for it?

The Three of Swords is an opportunity to reflect on our responses to inevitable and universal discomforts: loss, failure, criticism, stress. It can be a moment to step back and observe yourself, to put a little bit of distance between what's happened and how you're reacting to it. Feelings might be immediate, kneejerk, and unchangeable, but patterns of thought can be shifted. As the Austrian neurologist, psychiatrist and Holocaust survivor Victor Frankl is thought to have said, 'Between stimulus and response there is a space. In that space is our power to choose our response. In our response lies our growth and our freedom.'

This card does not suggest that pain or trauma is somehow edifying. Instead, it acknowledges that difficult things over which you have absolutely no control can happen, and that they can change you. The Three of Swords encourages you to recognise your pain. And it invites you – when you're ready – to do something with your story. Perhaps that means sharing it with a person or community who can help you to heal. Perhaps it means sharing it to help someone else feel less alone.

It's not always easy to see the gift in the Three of Swords, particularly when you're in the thick of it, but it's there. It warns you not to ignore pain and let it fester, or to be afraid of it and try to push it away. Whenever I see this card, I think of the Japanese practice of kintsugi, in which broken pottery is repaired with veins of golden lacquer. The object is restored to wholeness, but the cracks that reveal its history aren't hidden away. They're part of it.

Like a sword tempered by the flame, your mind can be honed by your experiences. The Three of Swords isn't a card of breaking. It's a card of forging anew.

QUESTIONS TO ASK WHEN YOU SEE THIS CARD: **Are you in pain?** How have you been wounded in your life? How has that pain changed you? How do you respond to being hurt? Is there an old wound that you still need to address? How can you take time to rest and heal, away from processing these emotions?

FOUR OF SWORDS

There are some cards in the tarot that we're always happy to see. And here, nestled among the sharp edges and increasingly difficult conversations of the Swords, is one of them. The Four of Swords, for once, isn't about wielding blades – it's about putting them down. This is the card of hanging up your weaponry and having a little rest. That's what you'll see illustrated on most cards: someone having a lie down, sleeping peacefully surrounded by their beloved swords. This, my friends, is the tarot card of the nap.

(If you're reading from the Rider Waite Smith, don't be

alarmed by the illustration. I'm not going to pretend to you that it isn't a picture of a tomb. I will not say 'he's not dead, he's just sleeping' like he's a goldfish and you're a five-year-old. I will simply remind you that the tarot isn't squeamish about death – and what is death, anyway, if not the ultimate big nap?)

Now, I'm no biologist, but I think you'll agree that sleep is an important activity. Forget 'I'll sleep when I'm dead' – it turns out that if you don't sleep, you will literally die (who knows, maybe that's what happened to our entombed knight). Sleep is a fundamental biological process, one that keeps you physically and psychologically well. When this card appears, it can simply be a moment to ask about whether you're getting enough rest. Do you have the downtime that you need: the periods when you're allowed to switch off and let your brain regroup? We spend all day, every day, bombarded by thousands of thoughts and sensory experiences. If you don't get the opportunity to rest, you don't have the chance to process and make sense of them all. The Four of Swords is a reminder that a crucial part of caring for yourself is taking that time out.

Sleep is the most obvious route to downtime – and arguably the most universal experience for the tarot to draw on. But, really, this card has a place in any practice that allows you to carve out space for yourself. Mindfulness wasn't exactly a huge trend in Western Europe when the tarot was invented, and neither were yoga studios, watching Netflix in the bath, meditation apps, pottery classes, or, indeed, doing any kind of crafting as a tool for relaxation rather than as a means of subsistence. But that was then, this is now, and so wherever and however you find ways to quieten your busy mind, the Four of Swords is on board. Whatever your reason, however acute or benign the need, this card is a reminder to take the time to do the things that give you that sense of calm. Resting isn't a reward; it's a necessity.

This card can also occasionally speak to the experience of just feeling quite bored. There can be times, even when you're very busy on an energetic level, when your mind is under-stimulated, foggy, and disengaged. Some jobs are like that. So is much of the daily business of parenting. In the Four of Swords, the tarot offers up an answer to that feeling too – though, depending on your circumstances, it might be easier said than done. 'A change is as good as a rest!' it says, breezily. Thanks, Four of Swords. You're not wrong.

QUESTIONS TO ASK WHEN YOU SEE THIS CARD: How do you switch off? What can you do to clear your mind and rest? Are you getting enough downtime? Are you bored or under-stimulated intellectually? Do you need a change?

FIVE OF SWORDS

CONFLICT, COLDNESS, OTHERNESS, LACK OF EMPATHY,
DOUBLE STANDARDS, DEFEAT

Traditional interpretations of this card will tell you that it's about having a disagreement with someone, which it certainly is. But, like all of the tarot, you really unlock its true usefulness when you let it go big. The Five of Swords isn't just about an individual disagreement; it's about the *concept of disagreement* – with anyone and, potentially, everyone. Specifically, it's those moments when we are so convinced that we have it right that anyone who doesn't agree with us, anyone who questions us, becomes The Enemy. They are worthy of nothing but our scorn and disgust. We are happy to go for the jugular. It's an exercise in allowing pure intellect to reign, with all of its deadly edges unsheathed, razor-sharp, and glittering.

This style of argument is far from rare, and plenty of us exhibit it in even our most minor, day-to-day quibbles (you'll see it again in the Knight of Swords). But you see it most often when the people who are disagreeing with one another don't have any kind of connection – when it's an argument with the anonymous, the other, or, worst of all, 'the public'. Fellow feeling is hard to preserve when you're dealing with strangers, particularly when they're ones with different opinions, beliefs, or voting tendencies. You don't know them so, occasionally, you find yourself deciding that they are all awful, and deserve every ounce of vitriol that you can throw at them. As the author Megan Nolan wrote in an article for *The Guardian*: 'the individual credits himself with complex and justifiable motivations even when wrongdoing takes place, and ascribes stupidity and wickedness to strangers who behave identically.' We sometimes forget that other people are human, too, and fail to offer them the compassion that we'd want for ourselves.

This is a dangerous path to tread when it comes to disagreements. You might win your argument, but at what cost? The Five of Swords asks us to be wary of those moments when you lose your capacity for empathy. Even when your opponent is universally agreed to be an awful person with hateful views, even when you are absolutely right in standing up to them and making yourself heard, you win nothing by dehumanising them. The Five of Swords is an opportunity to think about your approach to conflict and debate. How do you handle yourself? Do you serve respect and compassion with your intellect?

Of course, there are two sides to every argument, and for every victory there is a defeat. This card doesn't just raise questions about how you behave towards people you disagree with – it also invites you to examine how others have behaved towards you. Perhaps you've been on the pointy end of someone else's conversational swords recently. Or perhaps you're being attacked more profoundly and painfully: by an ideology or school of thought that denies your personhood, or runs roughshod over something that you hold dear. We all know the saying about treating others as you'd like to be treated yourself, but there's nothing that makes the blood boil quite like being treated badly. It can make you want to give as good as you get. Sometimes, other people really are the worst, and this card acknowledges that truth. But it also asks you to do better, to hold on to your humanity – especially when it feels toughest.

QUESTIONS TO ASK WHEN YOU SEE THIS CARD: How do you handle yourself in an argument? Do you succumb to double standards? How do you deal with opponents who you don't know personally? Have you felt attacked or othered in a conflict?

SIX OF SWORDS

TRANSITION, PROCESSING, TRAUMA,
RELEASING BAGGAGE, RESISTANCE

The Six of Swords speaks to a time of transition: specifically, the point at which you begin to move on from something that has been difficult or turbulent, and into a calmer and more positive state of mind. When it appears, it tends to bring up periods in life or specific events from which people struggle to release themselves, and which, in all likelihood, have left their mark. This card cares less about the details of what happened, and more about the process of working through it. More than anything, the Six of Swords asks what you've learnt from an experience: what will you take from it, and what have you left in the past? How does this event influence your present, and how might it shape your future?

The Six of Swords doesn't make assumptions about the scale of the thing that has caused difficulty. It's just as applicable to a casually cruel remark that you turn over in your head for days or a moment when you feel like you failed at something and let the side down as it is to a sustained period of stress or sadness. The event itself may have been large or small: the card doesn't point to any particular reason or time frame; it points to the weight of it in a querent's mind. As is often the case with the Swords, it's worth being sensitive to the potential for this card to bring up experiences that are significant, emotive, or traumatic.

This card is also a reminder that the work of processing difficult events is rarely easy, and even more rarely linear in fashion. Sometimes there are regular steps forward, and sometimes you stall. There are few signposts in this strange new world. For me, the Six of Swords brings up the year that followed a dear friend ending her life: a year in which I often felt like I was losing my own mind. The initial shock and pain of her loss rapidly became a grief which should, theoretically, have led to a chance for me to let her go. But I didn't. I wanted to stay in limbo, because moving forward felt like I was giving up on her. By staying in the same psychological place that I had been in when I found out that she had died, I felt like I could stay closer to her. Her death was a problem that I was trying to solve and to somehow make right. It took a long time for me to understand how impossible that was, and to loosen the reins on my grief.

There's a line in Carmen Maria Machado's *In The Dream House* which I think captures the lesson of this card: 'Just because the sharpness of the sadness has faded does not mean that it was not, once, terrible. It means only that time and space, creatures of infinite girth and tenderness, have stepped between the two of you, and they are keeping you safe as they were once unable to.' The Six of Swords says that, eventually, painful experiences stop feeling like splinters lodged beneath the skin. You don't need to have an answer to your pain in the moment that it happens. You simply need to let time carry you onwards.

QUESTIONS TO ASK WHEN YOU SEE THIS CARD: What have past experiences taught you? How do you process difficult experiences? Are you able to let go of things that don't serve you? Is there anything that you're struggling to move through?

SEVEN OF SWORDS

LYING, DECEPTION, DECEIT, CONCEALMENT, BETRAYAL,
SELF-PROTECTION, BIDING YOUR TIME

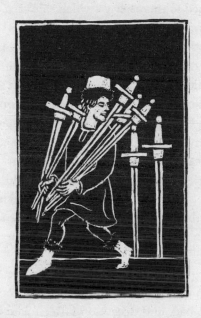

By this point in the suit, you'd be forgiven – no, correct – for
thinking that, as a rule, fewer swords is better. How strange,
then, to encounter a card in which a figure seems to be actively
acquiring more swords. In fact, he is stealing them. This villain
is pulling off the greatest sword heist of our generation, using
trickery and loose clothing to conceal his actions! Indeed, the
most straightforward interpretation of this card is deceit and
duplicity, and the simplest approach to its appearance in a
reading is to ask about it. Is there something going on? Who
are you lying to and what are you lying about? How many

swords have you stolen? What did you do with them? Where are they hidden?

The problem with this approach is that, as a tarot reader, it's not actually your job to be an interrogator. It's the querent who seeks answers, not you. What's more, very few people enjoy being accused of lying. And if they aren't lying, or don't think they're being lied to themselves (which this card can also indicate), you're probably going to get their hackles up if you push that interpretation. To use the Seven of Swords as such a blunt instrument is to miss the point. The question isn't whether deception is taking place in someone's life – let's be honest, it invariably is in one way or another. The question is *why*.

More often than not, lies are protective: they're a defence against a perceived threat, and that's what you should be examining. The threats could turn out to be shadows, rather than monsters – the Swords are the suit of the mind, after all, and the mind plays tricks – but they're clearly provoking a response. So, what is it that your querent is responding to? Why don't they feel that they can be honest with other people – or perhaps with themself?

The Seven of Swords can nudge you to see things from a different and more generous perspective. Generally, lying is assumed to be bad, and deception is seen as a moral failure. But there are plenty of situations where not being truthful is very much the best approach. The Seven of Swords is in those moments when your facial expression or your words do not match what you actually think. If we all just walked around being totally candid all the time, the results would be disastrous. Sometimes we have to be polite. Sometimes it's fine – expected, even – to just play along.

And sometimes, dishonesty is a way of creating space for yourself that you desperately need. Anyone who has needed to leave a toxic situation knows very well that telling their tormentor what they are planning is not a good idea – it's best to operate under cover of darkness. The same can be true of new ideas and projects that aren't yet ready to be shared more widely. The Seven of Swords can speak to times when you're working on or towards something that you haven't told anyone about, not because you plan to keep it a secret forever, but because it's not ready to be introduced to the world just yet.

This card creates space to ask – gently – about the difference between what someone chooses to reveal, and the whole truth of the matter. But what it doesn't do is claim that one is necessarily better than the other.

QUESTIONS TO ASK WHEN YOU SEE THIS CARD: Do you feel like you can be honest with yourself and others? Do you feel others are honest with you? What are you hiding, and are you hiding it for good reason?

EIGHT OF SWORDS

ENTRAPMENT, PANIC, INSECURITY, PESSIMISM, FEAR, ADDICTION,
NEGATIVE PATTERNS, PERSONAL AGENCY, CONTROL

We have both tried, for many years, to come up with a better
and more sophisticated analogy for the Eight of Swords, but
there's only one that really works. It is being TRAPPED IN A
GLASS CASE OF EMOTION. This is the card of being stuck,
weeping, in a phone box, in the film *Anchorman*. You want out.
You call for help but nobody seems to hear you or understand.
You're miserable because it feels like you have no choice but to
remain in this place.

This can be a difficult card to see in a reading. In most
decks, it is depicted by a figure who stands, blindfolded and

curled in on herself, in the centre of a ring of swords that are stabbed into the ground like prison bars. At its darkest, it's an image that conjures a sense of panic and desperation: being victimised or trapped in a cycle of self-destruction, and feeling as though no one can or will come to help you. Even in its softest voice, it speaks to sadness, to feeling muffled and separated from the world. It reminds me of a page in Shaun Tan's sensitive exploration of depression, *The Red Tree*, in which he illustrates the feeling that 'wonderful things are passing you by' with an image of the book's protagonist gazing out of a locked window at a huge and exquisite paper bird floating through a sunset sky.

Someone experiencing an Eight of Swords moment is probably not at their best. They might be quiet and withdrawn. Or they might be lashing out blindly and painfully like a caged animal. The Eight asks you to offer compassion and patience for whoever finds themselves in the ring of swords. If it's someone else, that doesn't mean allowing yourself to be treated badly, or failing to set boundaries and assert your own needs. But it does mean remembering that sometimes it is far easier to see a solution when you're not the one in the depths of the problem. It can be frustrating to watch someone you know and love struggle: to wonder why they can't just snap out of it, especially when you know that *if they could just do this* (whatever *this* is) it'd all be fine. You might be right, but they need to come to it in their own time. It's one of the oldest and truest clichés: you can't help people who aren't ready to help themselves.

And if the person experiencing the Eight of Swords is you, then the hardest lesson but also the greatest gift of the cards is the same one: it's that the power to change is within you. In most decks, you can see that there's a gap in the ring of swords wide enough that the trapped figure could walk out of it. You can retrain your brain. The glass case of emotion has a working door with a handle. The beautiful red tree of life is always waiting, quietly, for you to notice it again, and to come back to it. The Eight of Swords is a reminder that, no matter how cruelly your brain is trying to convince you otherwise, you hold the keys to the prison – not in your hands, but in your mind. It might not be easy to leave, but it is possible.

QUESTIONS TO ASK WHEN YOU SEE THIS CARD: Are you feeling trapped? Are there things that make you miserable, but which seem to be beyond your control? Why do you believe that you can't change the situation? Are you sure there's no way out? Can you ask for help?

NINE OF SWORDS

ANXIETY, FEAR, SLEEPLESSNESS, WORRY, ISOLATION,
NIGHTMARES, CANDOUR

The Nine of Swords is the card of anxiety. Most decks depict it
with an image of night dreads: awakening in the small hours,
paralysed by fears and worries which are, would you believe it,
represented by nine swords hanging above the bed. The Spolia
Tarot takes a more fantastical approach in which hoofed beasts
and winged demons awaken a woman from her slumber. In
the Wild Unknown deck, there's something altogether more
gruesome: maggots and worms writhe among swords, eyeballs,
and a claw of some sort. The often surreal imagery has a point
to make: this card isn't about constructive worries or being

overwhelmed by your to-do lists. It's about those spiralling anxieties and fears that aren't necessarily rooted in reality; which are (ironically, given the metaphor of swords) kind of pointless.

Almost everyone has been here at some point: awake at 3am, feeling like the last person on earth, imagining the worst possible outcome for everything, and believing you're unable to do anything about it. This card might refer to a specific anxiety, something that's been bouncing around in your skull for a while, and which you've studiously avoided confronting. Or it could speak to an more indefinable feeling of unease with no obvious root cause. Either way, when it's a Nine of Sword kind of night, it isn't something that has a quick, practical fix. You can't just pat this one on the head and send it out to pasture. Unpicking the knot demands a different approach.

Often, the Nine of Swords speaks to the kinds of worries that begin with 'what if?' or 'if only . . . ': the kinds that pull you back to the past, or try to peer into an uncertain future. This is not a healthy game to play, but it's also a hard one from which to extricate yourself. One way to interrupt the spiral is to draw your observations back into the present: how are you right now? What is actually happening today? What is true? This card is a reminder that you are not your thoughts – you observe them, and you can change them. It takes work, but you can choose to challenge the narrative that your mind is presenting. Today, we know this technique as positive thinking, but it's been around for a long time. As Julian of Norwich, the fourteenth-century mystic and anchoress who lived in a small cell under a church through the worst visitation of the plague, wrote: 'All shall be well and all manner of things shall be well.' (She was fine.)

One of the most painful aspects of Nine of Swords moments is how lonely they feel. It's not easy to wrap words around the slippery reality of an anxious mind and convey what it feels like to others. Often people are afraid to peel back the facade of who they think they ought to be and reveal who they really are. But this card suggests that, hard as it is, if you were to share what you're going through, it might help. When the Nine appears in a reading, it can offer a querent the chance to break the silence and give voice to the anxieties that haunt them. Whether you're reading for yourself or for someone else, it can be a powerful reminder of the transformative magic of being truly heard.

QUESTIONS TO ASK WHEN YOU SEE THIS CARD: Are you feeling anxious? Are your worries constructive? Are you overwhelmed by them? Would you like to share them? How much of what you're worrying about is real, and how much is what you fear?

TEN OF SWORDS

DESPAIR, MISERY, ROCK BOTTOM, TRAUMA, SORROW,
ANGUISH, DRAMA, HOPE

Well, here it is. You've finally found it: officially the worst card
in the tarot. In almost every deck you'll find, it really, *really*
looks it, too. This card usually shows someone collapsed on the
ground with ten swords piercing their back – signifying misery,
ruin, and hitting rock bottom. Most people's instincts, quite
understandably, are to recoil from the image, to try to protect
themselves from what it's telling them.

This is the first lesson of the Ten of Swords: you need to
look at it and accept it for what it is. Lisa Sterle's Modern
Witch Tarot is particularly incisive on this. In her deck, there's

a second version of the card, in which the figure ignores the swords in her back while she plays with her phone. The card's name is replaced with the words 'EVERYTHING IS FINE'. Because it can be surprisingly easy to say that, can't it? It can be surprisingly easy to pretend things are fine when they are absolutely not. Given that this is the suit of the mind, it's impossible not to see this card's links to mental health. I have a long history of anxiety and depression and I've gradually come to realise that the thing that scares me more than anything else is having to admit to people how low I am feeling. There have been times in my life when everything was going wrong, when every time I turned there was a new body-blow and, even though I had supportive, loving people around me, I still found it impossible to confront the depths of my own despair. The Ten of Swords knows that sometimes the hardest part is actually admitting how bad it is.

It should go without saying, then, that when the Ten appears in a reading, sensitivity is needed. Just because a person says they're fine, it doesn't mean they are, and this card can open the floodgates. Even if you're reading for yourself, be gentle. The Ten is less about the moment that something stressful or traumatising happens, and more about your mind's response to it. Thoughts and fears and reactions to events can circle for a long time – years, even – before they finally come home to roost. Sometimes the Ten of Swords is the immediate result of one spectacularly awful week, day, or hour. Sometimes it's when things that have lain buried in your mind for far, far longer are finally exposed to the air.

Of course, this card certainly doesn't mean that your whole life is in tatters – it hits differently depending on where it turns up in a spread. It might refer to a specific aspect of life, or it might be something that a querent fears will happen. Once in a while, it turns up in such a way that the only possible interpretation is that somebody is being melodramatic ('I die! I am DEAD!'). But for the most part, it's a card that speaks to real pain and anguish, and it should be taken seriously.

The second lesson of the Ten of Swords is an easy one to miss, but a precious one. In the background of the card, beyond the jumble of swords, you can see the barest slice of sunlight peeking over the horizon. This card is a reminder that it's always darkest right before dawn. You can get through this. Just hold on.

QUESTIONS TO ASK WHEN YOU SEE THIS CARD: What's happened? Is there something you want to talk about? Are you actually fine or are you just saying that?

PAGE OF SWORDS

CURIOSITY, SPONTANEITY, SEIZING THE DAY, NEW OPPORTUNITIES,
NEW IDEAS, DISILLUSIONMENT, INHIBITION, FEAR

Ah, the Page of Swords. Usually the Pages offer little cause for
concern, but what we have here, essentially, is a child wielding
a deadly weapon. Now that they have it, there's no chance of
getting it off them. An outside observer would note a very real
danger of impalement, but the Page is fascinated: for them, the
sword is an exciting, appealing object, and one that is full of
potential. They have questions – many, many questions. Why is
it so sharp? What makes it shiny? They want to pick it up and
swing it around – *whoosh* – listen to that sound! What happens
if I do this? Just look at how it moves. Many of the other cards

in this suit represent states of mind that are jaded, concerned or tied up in knots, but the Page is a simpler creature. They're not worried by anything – just inquisitive about *everything*.

A Page of Swords matches their curiosity with the zeal of the newly converted. Expect them to be full of conviction about whatever it is that they've turned their mind to: it could be a new business idea, a hot take on an issue of the day, an obsession with a new hobby, a political opinion, or a direction in their life. They can't take their eyes off it! They're pretty certain their plan is flawless! And they won't put it down until they've thoroughly explored it, taken it to pieces, mastered it, or it's all ended in tears. (And even if it does, that's OK: failure isn't the enemy, and this Page knows how to learn from their mistakes.)

Depending on where you stand, this can be a refreshing, awe-inspiring attitude, or it can be downright terrifying. Perhaps you already recognise yourself in this character, or perhaps it's a part of you that you could do with channelling. This Page represents the joy of learning and experimentation; of coming at a problem out of left field; of forgetting what is cool or trendy and sticking with what fascinates you; or taking something old and seeing it as something new. It's a reminder of the importance of opening your mind, of letting ideas flow through you and accepting that some of them will be great and others completely . . . not. And this energy is absolutely vital in the creation of marvellous new things. How else do we innovate, learn, start businesses, meet outrageous deadlines, create inventions? The Page of Swords says just give it a go. They're like Henry Ford – the man who, when everyone said they needed faster horses, somehow went on to mass produce the car.

This passion comes at a cost – a Page of Swords thinks a lot. They can be dreamy and disconnected, which means they can get stuck in their own head, consumed by their thoughts. Their spirit is pure, but it's also fragile: it's all too easy for the world to write them off, to see them as silly, naive, or inexperienced and knock them back or ignore them altogether. When this card appears, it's a reminder that sometimes what ideas need to flourish isn't criticism and cynicism, it's a space and care. It's a teacher, a patient and gentle hand to help guide it on its way.

QUESTIONS TO ASK WHEN YOU SEE THIS CARD: Do you have a really good (/wild) idea? What is it? What's holding you back from pursuing it? How do you handle failure? Who could you ask for help, advice, guidance or mentorship?

KNIGHT OF SWORDS

DETERMINATION, QUICK-WITTEDNESS, ASSERTIVENESS,
REACTIVITY, FAILURE TO COMPROMISE

The Knight of Swords is someone with a very good brain. They have honed their mind to razor sharpness, and they know how to use it. They take arguments, thoughts and ideas, beliefs, and principles very seriously indeed, and use everything in their intellectual arsenal to advance their position. It's not enough just to have a point of view; they also tend to DESTROY all other lines of enquiry. This is the person who won't back down, and will not drop the argument until it is well and truly dead.

These can be incredibly powerful characteristics. Many high-achieving people have something of the Knight of Swords' ruthlessness and single-mindedness to them – and they use those qualities to do extraordinary things. At their best, this character is bold, direct, tenacious, and assertive: possessed of a nimble intellect and unparalleled debating skills. They certainly break a few eggs on the way to making an omelette, but don't always notice: there's no malice here, they're just focused on the task at hand. This Knight stands up for their truth, and is far more interested in getting to the right answer than in keeping people happy. There are those who might describe them as having something of the shark about them. But, as we should all know by now, sharks are both widely misunderstood and an extremely valuable part of the marine ecosystem. (And, really, what are a few test bites between friends?)

The shadow side of the card isn't hard to see. A Knight of Swords can be disruptive and hurtful, blunt, argumentative, and uncompromising – doing damage both to those around them and to themself. They have a tendency to see the world in binaries: are you friend or are you foe? Are you helping me or standing in my way? There's very little room for grey areas with a Knight of Swords. They can also be extremely self-righteous: if you cross them, you can be sure that you and whatever it is that you represent are as good as dead to them. The Knight of Swords' approach, at its worst, is that of Gore Vidal: it's not enough that I should succeed. Others must fail.

There are some environments and professions in which people actively cultivate the characteristics of the Knight of Swords (the one that most often springs to mind: barrister). Indeed, as an adult, it's an energy that you're more likely to encounter in work situations than in your personal life. But when you see this card, it's worth exploring where you sit on the spectrum of argumentativeness: do you live for the satisfaction of a well-matched verbal duel, or would you sell everything you own to avoid one? If someone disagrees with you, do you see it as a chance to learn or take it as a personal slight? There is something wonderful in the Knight of Swords' ability to let everything else fade away and just focus on the question at hand – but, to those who don't approach matters in the same way, their approach is less enjoyable.

It's fair to say that someone who entirely embodied the traits of the Knight of Swords might not be anyone's favourite person. But that doesn't mean their skillset isn't valuable, and that it shouldn't – under the right circumstances – be prized.

QUESTIONS TO ASK WHEN YOU SEE THIS CARD: How do you feel about arguments? Do you feel comfortable holding your own in a debate? Do you find it intimidating? Do you have a tendency to win at all costs? Can you be too blunt?

QUEEN OF SWORDS

CLARITY, WIT, INTELLECT, CANDOUR, TRUTH,
DIRECTNESS, COLDNESS, BRUTAL HONESTY

Of the four tarot Queens, this is the one who feels the least comfortable for many people. It signifies directness and clarity of thought unencumbered by self-doubt or anxiety. It's someone who leads with the head rather than the heart, and never shies away from the truth. They don't pander to others or soften their words, and thus can be seen as cold, distant, and aloof. Like all of the figures of the tarot, it's not tied to a specific gender and doesn't have to represent a woman. But I think there is something very important – something telling – in the fact that the discomfort people feel with this card has far more to do with it being portrayed as female than the traits it represents.

If you're looking for feminine examples of Queens of Swords in fiction and popular culture, you can find them in abundance... but only in very specific places. They most often appear in myth and legend: as immortal goddesses, high fantasy elves, avenging angels, and ice queens. They are portrayed as uncanny and strange, unnatural – even horrific – in a way that a man who embodied the same characteristics wouldn't necessarily be. And so when this card appears, it's not simply a moment to ask a querent whom they recognise in her. It's also a moment to ask whether they believe her to be an acceptable aspect of someone's personality – including their own. Because she isn't always permitted to roam freely. Some people are allowed to be a little bit Queen of Swords, while others are immediately vilified for letting her out.

For me, this Queen always brings to mind a line about the mysterious, mythical presence released into the world by the protagonists of Alan Garner's *The Owl Service:* 'She wants to be flowers, but you make her owls. You must not complain, then, if she goes hunting.' There is nothing fundamentally sinister about the Queen of Swords, and she doesn't lack compassion. She is just what she has been made to be – and what she needs to be. She has a capacity for sharpness; she sees to the heart of things, doesn't suffer fools, and will skewer her enemies when she must. This Queen carries a blade, and she doesn't hesitate to use it to protect herself and others. Can we blame her if sometimes she has to do exactly that? Is it right to ask that people should always be soft and forgiving in the face of a world that can be pitiless and harsh? And isn't it strange that, generally, the people who are most consistently expected to exhibit softness are the same people who are most often the subjects of profound cruelty?

This is the card of wit and intellect, but it's also the card of brutal honesty, and of healthily expressed anger. A Queen of Swords doesn't hide things. They don't lie to you about what they believe, and they don't pretend they're not angry – whether that's about a slight, a mistake, or a grievous injustice. They wield their truth like a weapon: they can be a calm and collected ally, or a formidable opponent. The Queen of Swords is a natural and necessary energy in the deck and in the world. So, when she appears in a reading, she offers you a challenge. Will you look her in the eye and see her for who she truly is? And will you allow yourself to see your own face reflected in hers?

QUESTIONS TO ASK WHEN YOU SEE THIS CARD: Are you able to be direct and honest with people? Are you allowed to be angry? Are other people? What would happen if you stopped pretending?

KING OF SWORDS

WISDOM, EXPERTISE, INTELLIGENCE, TRUST, LEARNING,
EDUCATION, SUPERIORITY, SNOBBERY, KNOW-IT-ALL

The King of Swords is the card of intellectual authority. It represents expertise: someone who knows a lot about something, whether professionally, academically, or as a hobby. There is literally nothing you can't be the King of Swords about: astrophysics, lipstick shades, bird migration patterns, *Sex and the City* episodes, hard flooring, medieval art – it doesn't matter! The point of this card isn't the topic. The point is what it means to be knowledgeable and to be able to share your knowledge: to be, in a word, wise.

And what *does* it mean to be wise? Well, that's where things get tricky. As Shakespeare wrote, 'The fool doth think he is wise, but the wise man knows himself to be a fool.' There is a significant difference between being an intelligent person, and being a person who likes to pride themselves on being intelligent. Rigid thinking, defensiveness, and mansplaining are all in the shadow side of this King. It reminds us that the truly wise are prepared to admit to the things about which they know nothing, the things that make them feel incredibly stupid, and the questions that, even within their own field of expertise, they cannot answer. They know when to defer to others, when to listen and integrate experiences that are different to their own into their views. They want to be constantly challenged, and therefore to be constantly learning.

When you see the King of Swords, it's a chance to think about how this behaviour plays out in your life – both in your immediate surroundings, and more broadly. It can speak to times when you are right to be confident in yourself and your expertise: the feeling of having reached a point in your life where people turn to you because they believe that you are able to offer them good counsel. That's a position of significant responsibility, and one that can feel intimidating – because what if you get it wrong!? The King of Swords tells you that it's alright to not have all the answers, as long as you aren't afraid to admit to it; as long as you remain open-minded and aren't afraid of the unknown just because you don't know it.

It can also speak to times when people leverage perceptions of intellectual superiority to make others submit to them. 'I went to a Very Good University,' they say, 'which means that I am the cleverest, and therefore I am in charge.' Education is good. It opens doors to new ways of thinking about the world; it's the cradle of progress. But this card reminds us that it can be weaponised. If someone believes that they are owed deference just because of a particular phrase on their CV, then something has gone very rotten. (And if you're someone who does this... perhaps have a word with yourself.)

Expertise isn't claimed; it's earned. It's something that requires constant work. A good King of Swords isn't resting on their laurels, and they don't believe that they know it all, even if others consider them the ultimate authority in their field. They never lose their curiosity, never stop asking why and how, and wanting to know more. This is a beautiful energy to have. It's one that should always be appreciated and nurtured, in yourself and in others.

QUESTIONS TO ASK WHEN YOU SEE THIS CARD: What are you an expert in? When do people turn to you? Are you comfortable in that position? How are you using your wisdom, authority and platform? How do you keep on feeding your mind? Are you able to admit to things you don't know?

That very spiky run of Swords brings us to the end of the Minor Arcana. This means you're most of the way through the tarot: fifty-six cards down, only the twenty-two big ones to go!

Now, allow us to take this opportunity to make a (rare) prediction about you. We predict that most of the Minor cards are beginning to make sense to you now, but that there are some cards – sixteen, to be precise – which are still a bit of a mystery. The Pages, Knights, Queens, and Kings are the ones which are most easily confused with one another visually, and they do work in a slightly different way to the rest of the deck.

If our prediction is correct, rest assured that you're not alone: this is one of the more challenging aspects of learning the tarot for almost every reader. And so, before we move into the Major Arcana, we'll spend a little more time with these high and mighty personages, helping you understand these cards individually and together.

CHAPTER 8

Meet the Family

The court cards are also known as the families of the tarot and, like all of the best families, they're pretty weird. As you've seen, they don't have the helpful visual drama and storytelling of the numbered cards in the Minors: they're just sixteen extravagantly dressed people. So what on earth are you supposed to do when one turns up? Even worse, what happens if they arrive in a reading en masse? The most important thing is to remember that these are highly anthropomorphic cards. Their meanings are rooted in personality traits and quirks, rather than events or experiences. When they appear, the conversations they start are usually about characteristics and temperaments, natures and identities, virtues and vices.

Once you get to know them, you'll see how each of them is unmistakably an individual. The hard part is getting properly acquainted. Each set of four Pages, Knights, Queens, and Kings are all united by common traits (far more so than the number cards of the Minors). Their strengths and weaknesses, skills and blindspots, gifts and challenges are broadly consistent, which can make it harder to keep them separate in your mind. And so, to help you, we've prepared an overview of each – a sort of tarot job description, if you like – as well as some practical tips on reading them.

The Pages: Wild Children

One of the things you'll often read about the Pages of the tarot is that they are the messengers of the deck. I've always found this to be a profoundly unhelpful description – because what is the tarot if not a pack of messages? Every single card in that deck is trying to tell you something. Sometimes they even gang up on you, so that they can tell you twice or thrice. I can confidently say that 'messengers' is not the most straightforward shorthand for the Pages. But perhaps I can shed a little bit of light on where this notion comes from, and what it might more usefully and practically mean for your readings.

In a 1986 interview, Maurice Sendak, author of *Where the Wild Things Are*, shared an anecdote which I think speaks very powerfully to the Pages' energy. He recounted an occasion when he responded to a letter from one of his young readers by sending a postcard on which he had drawn a Wild Thing. He received thanks from the child's mother, who told him that the little boy had loved the postcard so much that he ate it. Sendak was delighted: 'That, to me, was one of the highest compliments I've ever received. He didn't care that it was an original drawing or anything. He saw it, he loved it, he ate it.' This is exactly how the Pages behave: unfiltered, unselfconscious, and gloriously untamed.

Indeed, the best place to start when it comes to understanding the Pages is to see them as the childlike characters of the tarot. They embody a youthful, naive, and therefore intuitive, approach towards the energy of their suits. Children, famously, are born not knowing how the world works. In childhood we gradually learn rules and structures, rituals and socially acceptable behaviours: we learn to become adults who can exist in a complicated and often confusing world. It is a fascinating process: children are endlessly curious, they love to play and puzzle things out, and they sometimes become obsessed with the strangest things. The Pages of the tarot do more or less the same thing: each of them comes at the energy of their suit without fear, concerned only with what they might be able to do, to make, or to become.

The thing about children, though, is that they are quite unusual little creatures, driven by very particular needs. As a society, we tend to idealise childhood and get misty-eyed about kids as beings of perfect grace, innocence, and possibility. But you shouldn't forget that the reason they are charming and curious and optimistic, entirely unhindered by ideas of how things should be, is that their brains are still developing. They are in a constant state of change and growth, and quite literally perceive the world differently to adults. There is increasing evidence from the scientific community that the effects of psychedelics are not dissimilar to returning the mind to a state of infant perception, when it was unencumbered by an understanding of how things are supposed to be and so can forge powerful new connections. This state can be magical: sometimes this means the invention of a spectacular new imaginary creature! But sometimes it leads to unexpected results: mixing yoghurt in your shoe. Innocence, it turns out, isn't always sweet, but it can be fruitful.

And this is absolutely how you should approach the Pages of the tarot. They represent people – or aspects of people's characters – who are still capable of wide-eyed wonder. They are imaginative (the Cups), questioning (the Swords), adventurous (the Wands), or just downright enthusiastic (the Pentacles). But that doesn't mean you can trust their judgement. The Pages are not yet worldly wise, they are not going to offer a carefully considered second opinion, and they definitely shouldn't be signing off expenses. Enjoy them for what they are, and bear in mind that, left to their own devices and without appropriate supervision, there's room for them to tip over from youthful exuberance into *Lord of the Flies* territory.

The purpose of the Pages is to remind us that these unfettered, uninhibited impulses live within all of us. We were all children once, and somewhere, deep in our psyches, the vestiges of that young mind still exist. When a Page appears in a reading, it might recall the people you know who take a youthful approach to the suit's energy. But it might also ask you to think about the childlike spirit within yourself: whether you still tend to it, whether you are kind and loving to it, and whether you still give it space to play, to make a mess, or to eat things it probably shouldn't. If the Pages are messengers, they're not from the outside world. When you see one, it's time to ask yourself whether perhaps the call is coming from inside the house.

The Knights: What a Ride

Like the Pages, the four Knights of the tarot have a natural association with the earlier phases of life – and are generally depicted as such in decks. But where the Pages embody childhood, the Knights represent the heightened intensity of adolescence. It would be far too reductive to describe them solely as 'teenagers'. But it is worth knowing that there's a traditional association between these characters and young adults, insofar as it can help you identify what parts of oneself and others they best represent when they appear in readings.

The basic rule of thumb for understanding the Knights of the tarot is that each of them takes the energy of their suit to its extreme. Whatever that energy is, they do it the absolute most. They give you supersized feelings in the Cups, sharp and furious clashes of minds in the Swords, passion to the point of obsession in the Wands, and – my personal favourite! – being so practical it's actually painful in the Pentacles. For that reason, when one of them arrives in a reading, the instinct is often to say, 'WOAH THERE, hold your horse, sir!' (obviously they all have horses). And that's not a bad instinct: you can have too much of literally anything. Sometimes the energy of the Knights is welcome because it gets things moving, but it's almost never a good idea to let something or someone run amok, unchecked and unbalanced.

A Knight in a tarot reading asks whether you're in the path of a seemingly unstoppable force, or whether you – or someone close to you – is taking something just that little bit too far. Is there something that needs to be reined in, or someone on whom you should be keeping a kindly, supervisory eye? The Knights point to activity and change, but also to getting ahead of yourself, of not thinking through the potential consequences, or of getting fixated on something and losing sight of the big picture. They can start conversations about specific people who are overwhelming a querent, making them feel cornered and panicked. As always with the tarot, if a card prompts a particular association, then that topic is worth investigating.

That all said, you should know by now that the tarot loves drama. And there is nobody – NOBODY – more plainly and unapologetically dramatic than its Knights. They are characters who are defined not by ideas and intentions, but by action. They are, in the most literal sense, actors. I don't necessarily mean they have big thespian vibes, but I also don't *not* mean that. Anne Carson wrote of actors, 'There is a theory that watching unbearable stories about other people lost in grief and rage is good for you – may cleanse you of your darkness. Do you want to go down into the pits of yourself all alone? Not much. What if an actor could do it for you? Isn't that why they are called actors? They act for you.' So much of the dramatic arts is about allowing an audience to witness, and in some ways experience, a story that's bigger than their own day-to-day experiences. It's about allowing them to access feelings and truths that would otherwise remain out of reach. The greatest actors are those who take you with them and make you see things entirely from their character's perspective. They allow you to inhabit the mind of someone else, even if only for a few moments.

And the Knights of the tarot, in their earnestness and sincerity and fervor, play a similar role. They might sometimes make you want to cringe so hard you turn yourself inside out, but they can also be agents of transformation, opportunities to understand something new about yourself, or about the world. They inhabit hyperbolic spaces and experiences; they turn a magnifying glass onto every tiny detail, and listen to every song with the volume turned up to the maximum. They will go there – no matter where 'there' is – at the drop of a hat, and they will squeeze everything they can out of it. It can be quite unnerving to encounter someone who feels comfortable in the extremes of life, but it can also be beautiful, and powerfully cathartic.

The Knights of the tarot are highly motivated, and bent on action. They aren't held back by embarrassment or shame – to be honest, the part of them that's capable of accurate self-reflection is absent. And there's no hard-and-fast rule about when they signify something that should be reined in, and when they're a call to run riot. But they always speak to a potential for intensity, in yourself or others, that cannot – and should not – be ignored.

The Queens: Being Oneself

One of the things I love about the Queens of the tarot (and there are many) is the fact that they are almost always depicted as mature women. It's rare to find a deck in which the Queens look like adolescents, or even as though they are in their twenties – they tend to be unapologetically middle-aged. Which is not to say that there's anything wrong with being younger. It's just that, as we all know, it's unusual to be presented with aspirational female characters who look as though they've actually lived.

With these characters, the fact that they've all got a good few years under their belts is crucial to understanding their power. When I think of the Queens, I am reminded of Susan Sontag's *The Double Standard of Ageing*, in which she explores the many ways in which women are encouraged to remain in a perpetual state of girlhood – both physically and behaviourally. At the end of the essay, she concludes that there is, perhaps, another option: 'They can aspire to be wise, not merely nice; to be confident, not merely helpful; to be strong, not merely graceful; to be ambitious for themselves, not merely for themselves in relation to men and children.' To me, the Queens are the embodiment of this other path: this embracing of adult womanhood and centring of the self; the ability to understand one's place in the world on one's own terms, rather than relative to others.

While it goes without saying that the four Queens' being coded feminine doesn't mean that they have to represent women, I think rooting these symbols in feminine bodies speaks to something hard-won in their qualities. These are characters which have real gravitas, extraordinary self-knowledge, and a complex and nuanced understanding of the energies of their suits. And they didn't just wake up like that! These cards represent the culmination of study, practice, reflection, and experience. After the uncultivated optimism of the Pages and the forces of nature of the Knights, the Queens give us a moment of pause. They are still waters, but they run deep: gathering the energy of their suits close and cloaking themselves in their powers. One burns bright and brilliant, another offers up sharp, clear–sometimes brutal–truths. One holds a safe space for whispers of the heart, and another is anchored by deep roots into the solidity and sensations of the physical world. Each one not only understands her suit, she also acts as its guardian.

Like the rest of the cards, the Queens all have their less agreeable sides. In keeping with the general tone (and central symbol) of each of the suits, the Queens of Swords and Wands have rather more potential to be spiky and bruising than the Queens of Pentacles and Cups, who, at their worst, tend towards materialism and docility, respectively. On the whole, though, when these cards show up in a reading they're not here to cause trouble. I would never advise completely letting your guard down with them – the tarot is nothing if not full of surprises! – but generally, when one of these grand dames emerges for a turn around the room, it's a 'when you hear hooves, think horses, not zebras' moment: the more benevolent interpretation is probably the correct one.

Something that can make the Queens difficult to read, particularly when you're starting out, is that they don't tend to speak to action. They aren't really asking you to do anything, or even necessarily to change your perspective. Each Queen is more of a mood than a direction. For much the same reason, I've often noticed that, of all the court cards, these are the ones that people tend to find easiest to identify as friends, acquaintances, or family members: people they admire, or look up to. This can be a useful avenue to explore: these cards often allow us to reflect on the networks of support and strength that hold us up. But it can also be worth really probing how a Queen card relates to your own sense of self. Do they live within you? Do you wish they did?

There aren't all that many words in English that refer to

strong, adult women in a positive fashion. In fact most, even the ones that started out as compliments, or at least neutral, factual descriptors – virago, matron, beldam – have managed to pick up disparaging, sneering stains over time. Queen is one of the only ones left, and there's something quite wonderful in the way that it's taken on a new life as a gender-neutral term of approval. In the modern world, queens are people who know who they are, what they are made of, and what they're capable of. And the tarot's Queens are a way of asking: do you know too?

The Kings: Big (Suit) Energy

There is a series of books which has been very dear to my heart since I first read them nearly twenty-five years ago, and which ended up being the key to understanding the Kings of the tarot for me: Tamora Pierce's magical medieval Tortall novels. Their protagonists are all warrior maidens but, in the foundational quartet, *The Song of the Lioness*, the secondary character is a prince whose journey is one of learning how to shoulder the burden of leadership: how to put aside his own desires and grow into a ruler who will do right by his people. We meet him again and again over the course of a dozen books and two things are firmly established: first, that he becomes an excellent monarch who brings about a golden age in his realm's history; and second, that many people think he's a bit of a prick. After meeting him, one young warrior solemnly observes that 'Maybe her father was right, and good kings weren't always good men.'

This, basically, is how you need to think about the Kings of the tarot. They are the very best at what they do, but that doesn't mean you're going to like them. Their actions are (or at least should be) guided by the greater good, and they play the long game. Each is the master of the energy of their suit:

knowing how to channel it and to bring it to bear on the world around them. They can be stern and dominating forces – even the most emotional, the King of Cups, represents a structure against which you can test yourself and discover your own boundaries. They're not trying to win you over. In fact, they aren't necessarily thinking of you at all – or at least, not 'you' as an individual with hopes and needs and wants and desires separate from a collective. Their purpose isn't to make you fond of them; it's to do what needs to be done.

And the thing about that is that you kind of have to respect it. There is courage and conviction in not minding if people like you, in living by your principles and being able to sacrifice some personal comforts in service of your ideals. If you're thinking about a King as representing someone in your life, it's likely to be someone who's influential or has authority over you. So, when they appear, the Kings often invite you to consider how you interact with those kinds of characters. Are you in awe of them? Do you find them intimidating? Do you resent the fact that they don't really seem to see you, that their gaze is set on the horizon? Is it alright if you don't always like them?

The questions become all the more pointed when you think about the Kings as aspects of yourself – particularly as aspects which you might be repressing. Are there times when you make yourself smaller or more submissive because you're afraid of what people might think if you didn't? Could you live with the idea of someone being angry, annoyed, upset, or frustrated with you if it were in service of doing what you knew was right? Like the Queens, the Kings of the tarot are intrinsically motivated, drawing their sense of purpose and fulfilment from within rather than looking for external validation. But their actions tend to cast a longer shadow, and they're far more closely identified with the trappings of worldly achievement: the expert, the visionary, the patriarch, and the tycoon. Those identities don't always sit comfortably with people, and it can be hard to acknowledge that they might have a place somewhere within your own sense of yourself.

The counterpoint to the notion that good kings aren't always good people (although some are both), is that bad kings are, without a doubt, absolutely dreadful. The shadow sides of the tarot's Kings play like an almost comical line-up of villains: the abuser and master manipulator; the billionaire hoarder watching the world go hungry from their palace; the intellectual elitist who can't see the value in anyone who doesn't share their background; the megalomaniac who probably spends all their time trying to go to space. It would be nice to think that these kinds of people don't exist but, obviously, they do. In these cards, the tarot gives us a chance to acknowledge how difficult and damaging such people can be as they stomp around in their big, Bad King boots, as well as offering a cautionary tale to anyone who might be heading that way themselves.

Ultimately, when a King appears, it's important not to jump to conclusions. They aren't always the easiest characters on a personal level, but they are the engines of their suit, using its raw energy to power their life's work. Sometimes, they are exactly what's needed.

Courtly Etiquette

Hopefully by now the differences between the court cards are clearer. But there are also some techniques that can help you to fix them in your mind, and interpret them confidently in a reading.

On a practical level, the first thing you should do when a court card rides into a reading is to ask whether they feel familiar. Do you recognise this figure? Do they remind you of anyone? A court card could be a friend, a family member, a colleague – anyone at all. I know we've mentioned this in the descriptions of each of the cards, but it bears repeating: don't let the traditional naming conventions of these cards limit your idea of who they might represent. Just because the card is, for example, a Queen, that doesn't mean it has to represent a powerful woman. It would be wrong to say that you should simply ignore the trappings of masculinity and femininity that these cards play with – in fact, it can be very helpful to use that as a lens to explore the nuances of their meanings. But never treat them as fixed binaries, or forget that people of any and all genders can embody the characteristics of any and all of the court cards.

Indeed, while the Rider Waite Smith and many other traditional tarot decks don't always make it easy to embrace the universality of these cards, there are other modern decks that do things differently. They offer alternative ways of describing the four court positions, which you might find helpful in unpacking each archetype's role in the suit. The Tarot of the Crone by Ellen Lorenzi-Prince, for example, explores the power of the older woman and renames the cards the Beast, Witch, Grandmother, and Shadow. The Numinous Tarot by Cedar McCloud reimagines the King and Queen as Mystic and Creator. Ari Wisner brings us the Transient Light Deck, recasting the court with the Crown, Keeper, Champion, and Apprentice.

If the court cards don't remind you of someone you know, there's another very significant angle to consider. Sometimes, they invite the gaze to be turned inwards. We like to think of a court card as representing a person who's exerting a powerful influence on your life . . . and who has a greater impact on your life than, well, you? With that in mind, a valuable exercise when you're trying to get to grips with these cards is to write down how you relate to each of them. When have you embodied the Page of Cups? What does a Knight of Wands moment look like for you? These are all different facets of the self and, while some might be more dominant than others, it's a rare person who doesn't have a little bit of every single one somewhere in themself.

When it comes to really getting to know the subtle differences between the court cards, we suggest doing what you might if you were meeting actual people: sitting them down round a table and asking questions. Try drawing all sixteen cards and pulling them in pairs. What would the Page of Wands have for breakfast and what would the Queen of Swords have to say about that? How would the Knight of Cups handle a breakup compared to the Knight of Swords? What could the Page of Pentacles teach us about change and what would the King of Cups do differently? Perhaps imagine a fabulous imaginary dinner party for them. Which cards would sit next to whom? Who would make sparkling conversation? (The Queen of Pentacles would be charming.) Who would never get invited back again?

CHAPTER 9

Major Behaviour

If you've come across any tarot cards before, chances are it's these ones. The Major Arcana are the trump cards of the deck, and I like to think of them as its misunderstood celebrities. Popular culture is peppered with images from the tarot – everyone has seen a film or TV show in which The Lovers, The Hanged Man, or Death (of which, as you may know from *Father Ted*, 'There's only meant to be one in each pack!') appears. Nine times out of ten, the fictional tarot reader offers a spectacularly nonsensical omen of doom that fits the plot of the film, but bears no relation to the tarot. Once you've finished this chapter, you too will be able to be annoyed (or tickled) by how badly these cards are misrepresented!

Major Arcana literally means 'big secrets' and the appearance of these cards in a reading invites us to talk about the seismic shifts we experience in life. But don't take them at face value. This is where you must hold fast to the knowledge that the cards of the tarot are not literal, and rarely mean what you think they do. Welcome to Metaphor Town, population: twenty-two. The card with a pregnant lady on it does not mean you're about to have a baby. The Devil has very little to do with Satan. The Lovers? Not actually a prediction of relationship success (sorry). In our experience, it's particularly important to labour this point with anyone you're reading for when one of the more alarmingly named cards appears – everyone feels better when you've reassured them that you're not about to predict their untimely demise. You're not. In fact, you can't.

It's also crucial to remember that these are the most complex cards for a reader to interpret. They each have multiple layers of meaning, enfolded upon one another like the petals of a rose. Reading Majors means stepping through many levels of interpretation and trying each one on for size. And, rather than becoming simpler with practice, you'll instead find that there are new facets of each card to discover every time you encounter them.

While they might not always mean what they appear to resemble, it's fair to say that the twenty-two cards of the Major Arcana all have something important to say, something they want to tell you IN CAPITAL LETTERS. When it comes to feelings, they go large. Happiness is rendered so pure it's a naked baby on the back of a horse on a sunny day. Trouble is a tower being hit by lightning with people falling from its ramparts. Like the Minors, all of these cards have shadow sides – and sometimes those shadows are very long indeed. These are not cards that you can gloss over in a reading, or ones that add a little bit of padding and subtle shading to the spread. These are cards that demand to be seen and noticed.

This can be a little bit alarming – and it's why we recommend learning the Minor Arcana first. There are two-and-a-half times as many Minors in the deck as Majors so, between whatever powers of fate and fortune you ascribe to tarot readings, and pure statistical probability, you won't see them as often. The Majors almost always throw their weight around, changing the centre of gravity in a reading, or provoking some of the most candid and intimate conversations. But usually they appear flanked by Minors, which offer up the nuances and the gentler guidance, as well as providing a much-needed buffer between the querent and the Majors' complete lack of tact.

Sibling cards and suit associations

It can take time to learn how to read the relationships between the Major and Minor Arcana – although, with practice, it will become almost second nature. One useful thing to be aware of when you're starting out is that all of the Majors are aligned to one of the four elements of the Minor Arcana. Knowing which cards are associated with which element can help you to see the connections between them, and understand whether the Minor cards in a spread are amplifying, complementing, balancing out, or clashing with the energy of the Majors:

The cards of **water** (Cups) are The High Priestess, The Chariot, The Hanged Man, Death, and The Moon.

The cards of **fire** (Wands) are The Emperor, Strength, The Wheel of Fortune, Temperance, The Tower, The Sun, and Judgement.

The cards of **earth** (Pentacles) are The Empress, The Hierophant, The Hermit, The Devil, and The World.

And the cards of **air** (Swords) are The Fool, The Magician, The Lovers, Justice, and The Star.

In practical terms, this might mean that if you were to pull The Chariot – a card of willpower, determination, and forward momentum – and one of the Knights of the tarot, which are also very headstrong, you would have a clear sense that your querent is all about pursuing action. The Knight of Cups would amplify The Chariot's energy, for better or worse, leading to an interpretation about following your heart and your passion. The Knight of Swords would complement it, speaking to a marriage of heart and mind, indicating that the querent is bringing both of those fairly crucial aspects of the self to bear in their pursuit of a goal. The grounded, solid Knight of Pentacles would balance out some of The Chariot's charging energy, making it less of a wild ride, and more of a firm push in a direction that you know is right. And the Knight of Wands could feel like a worrisome addition to the party: a clash of water and fire that could be transformative, but is more likely to be a warning that something isn't right and the wheels are about to fall off.

There is no hard-and-fast rule about how different cards interact – and, in part, the reading depends on the context, the questions being asked, and the querent's own experiences. But you will find your readings more fulfilling (particularly with the Majors) if you can see the cards not as discrete, hermetically sealed objects, but as ingredients in a recipe. Some are more noticeable than others, but it's the relationships between them that create the magic. The cards of the tarot exist in dialogue with one another, sometimes supporting each other's messages, and sometimes adding a new lens or challenging assumptions. This is just as much the case between the Major Arcana as it is between the big cards and the Minors.

The Fool's journey

The cards of the Major Arcana follow a path which is numbered from 0 to 21. The position of each card in the deck, and the identities of its neighbours, can give additional context to its meaning. As the tarot scholar Rachel Pollack writes, 'each new trump builds upon the previous one and leads the way to the next'. The narrative arc of the twenty-two cards describes a hero's journey – the same story you'll have seen time and time again in fiction and film, in everything from *The Odyssey* to *The Neverending Story*, from *Star Wars* to *Mean Girls*.

The cycle begins with the infinite potential of The Fool (technically numbered as 0, which means that he could sit anywhere in the deck – the little rascal – and is the tale's protagonist) who takes a leap into the unknown as he sets out on a new adventure, full of hope and optimism. He finds friends, guides, and enemies along the way. He encounters obstacles which he must overcome. He experiences moments of joy and self-knowledge, as well as facing losses and dark nights of the soul. The final card in the Major Arcana is The World, in which the adventurer reaches the end of his journey, and can reflect on the lessons learnt, only for the cycle to begin once again.

You don't need to be able to remember the order of the Majors to start with, but it can be useful sometimes to know which cards are successive, and which cards are nearer to the beginning or the end of the sequence of twenty-two. The best example is the fairly dodgy patch in the middle, where you pass through The Hanged Man and Death, before a brief layover with inscrutable Temperance, and then on to The Devil and The Tower. The two neighbouring pairs are both difficult, and they both have relationships with one another. The Hanged Man is a card of birth, of sitting in a liminal space and deciding whether or not to step into transformation, while Death speaks to a change (or an ending) that is happening and will transform you whether you like it or not. The Devil is about being stuck in a pattern that can feel inescapable, while The Tower is about the sudden – often shocking – tumbling of structures that felt eternal and unassailable.

Then, right after this quartet of challenges and discomfort, you emerge into a wide, open sky: The Star, a card that symbolises hope, healing, stillness, and peace; The Moon, which is all about the unleashing of the subconsciousness (not always ideal, but liberating nevertheless); and then The Sun, which represents joy, a moment spent basking in the warmth of the light. This isn't a coincidence: the celestial cards are mature cards that offer you the chance to reflect on your experiences, to recognise that those experiences might not have been easy, and to decide how you feel about the whole thing. At the beginning of the sequence, you also get the nuptial pairing of The Empress and The Emperor, who are bookended by another masculine and feminine set in The High Priestess and the Hierophant. And at the very end, you have Judgement and The World, the former of which presages the latter, just as the Nines of the Minor Arcana hint at what's to come in the Tens.

Getting to know the Majors

You'll sometimes find compact tarot decks which only use the Major Arcana. It can be interesting to read from them, especially when you're in a 'go big or go home' kind of mood. One deck that we both enjoy on such days is Sophy Hollington and David Keenan's *The Autonomic Tarot*, a 30-card deck that adjusts the representations of some of the Majors, and also provides two cards for each Minor suit, to represent their extremities. Exploring readings in this way can be a valuable exercise. The Majors tell the story of the journey through life and they can exist as a self-contained narrative, populated with archetypes that we all carry within ourselves and experience to a greater or lesser extent. They don't pull their punches, but they have important stories to tell.

The greatest challenge with this section of the tarot is the complexity of potential meaning within these cards. Each of them lends itself to multiple levels of interpretation, and most readers develop personal associations with all of them – some cards they love, some they hate to see, and almost all of them freighted with meanings derived from their own experiences. For every person who has an intuitive understanding of a particular card, there's someone else who really struggles to get their head around it: these cards are impossible to distill into pure essence, or crystallise into a solid form. The key to learning and enjoying them is to allow yourself to explore all their hidden depths, challenges, and gifts: to embrace, rather than be daunted by, the fact that each of them contains multitudes.

CHAPTER 10

The Majors

O The Fool
I The Magician
II The High Priestess
III The Empress
IV The Emperor
V The Hierophant
VI The Lovers
VII The Chariot
VIII Strength
IX The Hermit
X Wheel of Fortune
XI Justice
XII The Hanged Man
XIII Death
XIV Temperance
XV The Devil
XVI The Tower
XVII The Star
XVIII The Moon
XIX The Sun
XX Judgement
XXI The World

THE FOOL (O)

Nobody likes to be called a fool in day-to-day life and that's fair enough. The tarot, however, operates by a different set of rules. Here in the land of the cards, pulling The Fool is far from an insult.

As the first card of the Major Arcana, The Fool represents the starting point of the journey of life. They are the unformed self, setting out on a big adventure free from prejudices and prior experiences that shape their expectations. As a result, in the Rider Waite Smith, they are depicted doing something that looks like it might be a very bad – perhaps even foolish – idea:

they are about to walk off the edge of a cliff. But they're fine! Despite the laws of physics, they're not plunging to their death! The essence of The Fool is the purest optimism, and their gift is the power of taking risks and venturing into the unknown in pursuit of your desires.

Whenever this card appears, it asks you to consider where your heart is leading you, and whether you are holding yourself back when you needn't. Is there a project, a connection, an idea that you want to explore but which you've told yourself is silly and unrealistic? Well, The Fool doesn't believe in the word 'silly'. Is there something that you want to do but are afraid to try – something that you fear could fail and leave you hurt and sad? The Fool reminds us that, unfortunately, there is no way to avoid hurt and sadness in life – they go hand in hand with joy, the shadow to its light. Is there something you will only allow yourself when, if, once; *mañana, mañana*? The Fool says the time is now. They believe that the worst possible thing is to live in grey, afraid to try because you might not succeed. They believe that the reward of glorious technicolour is worth the risk.

Fools are a well-established archetype. In literature, they are often prophetic, able to see more clearly and speak more truly than those around them. Shakespeare's court jesters' positions outside the social hierarchy permits them to comment upon it, offering up insight coded in riddles and the opportunity to alter the order of things. Robin Hobb's many-faced Fool flits at will from male to female identities, sometimes capering and sometimes serious, but always working to nudge those around him/her off course and into action that will make the world a better place. It's worth remembering that this character isn't an entirely naive one. The Fool embodies youthful optimism, but that doesn't mean they don't have a purpose, or that their purpose cannot be lofty. This card can speak to dreams and ideals that seem beyond your reach, asking you: are they really such a stretch?

You never know what lies ahead. But if you allow yourself to be held back by fears and what ifs, you'll also never get to find out. It isn't easy to put yourself out there, to take risks, to wear your heart on your sleeve, or to leap and hope that someone or something will catch you. But The Fool reminds us that doing so is brave, and often necessary. This card reminds us that hope isn't foolish at all.

QUESTIONS TO ASK WHEN YOU SEE THIS CARD: Are you ready to take a leap? Are you hesitating on the precipice of something new? What are you hoping for? What are you afraid of? Isn't it better to try than to hold yourself back?

THE MAGICIAN (I)

ENERGY, DETERMINATION, MANIFESTATION, LACK OF FOCUS,
MISUSE OF POWER, MANIPULATION

The Magician goes by many names: seer, shaman, prophet,
fairy godmother, wizard, or even sometimes one of the gods.
In *The Hero with a Thousand Faces*, Joseph Campbell calls
this archetype 'the Mentor with Supernatural Aid'. Film, culture, and literature are replete with examples: King Arthur
has Merlin; Dorothy has Glinda the Good Witch; Harry Potter
has Dumbledore; Peter, Susan, Edmund, and Lucy have Aslan;
Link has Princess Zelda; the Karate Kid has Mr Miyagi; Neo
has Morpheus; your authors have their agent; you have this

card. The idea here is simple – you are on a quest and The Magician is here to help.

Usually, then, he's a welcome guest in a reading. The Magician can help you turn the ordinary into the extraordinary, dreams into reality, the impossible into the completely possible. He is a lightning rod, connecting the heavens and the earth, the macrocosm to the microcosm, the subconscious and the conscious. He harnesses the powers of the universe and manifests that energy however he pleases. You could call it a trick but, really, The Magician represents the privilege of confidence, whether that comes from education, wealth, love, someone having your back, or special guidance. This is a card that frees you to express your highest vision. He has the ultimate superpower: of not being encumbered by self-limiting beliefs.

Often this card is rendered male but, to me, it also brings to mind Jerry Hall: model, Texan, iconic blonde. Many Christmases ago in a newspaper column, she gave advice to readers on how to endure the party season. 'It's a service to your fellow guests to arrive in a fabulous way,' she said. On entering a room, look across it and wave at a far corner, as though you've spotted someone you know, and then march off in that direction. It is quite the statement. Truly, this is a Magician in her element.

When this card appears, it opens up questions of how and if you feel able to confidently channel yourself into what you want to achieve. You might recognise yourself in The Magician, or it might feel like a completely alien energy to you. Usually this card is an invitation to believe in yourself, to be bold and fearless and act on your ideas and goals as though you have a direct line to the heavens. Of course, there are also times when you might need to power down a little. You're probably not the only wizard around and, although this town might well be big enough for all of you, you could find sparks flying if no one will make any concessions. How can you share your gift? How can you make space for others?

The Magician represents an alignment of effort, intention, and the right conditions. It's about bringing all aspects of yourself to bear and approaching a problem or an opportunity as an integrated whole: mind, body, heart, and soul (accordingly, in many decks, The Magician is shown surrounded by the four Aces of the Minor Arcana). This self-knowledge and strength of conviction is nothing to be ashamed of: it's a powerful arsenal, and one that can be channelled into great achievement.

QUESTIONS TO ASK WHEN YOU SEE THIS CARD: What is your goal? What is your motivation? Are you confident in yourself? Are you overbearing? What is the greatest obstacle you face? Who do you look up to, and how might you make a little of their sparkle yours?

THE HIGH PRIESTESS (II)

MYSTICISM, INTUITION, INSTINCT, PERCEPTION, MAGIC,
IRRATIONALITY, DENIAL

The High Priestess speaks to mysticism in its most traditional sense: an ability to peer beyond the veil, past the surface of things, and access hidden truths. She is powerfully identified with the supernatural, psychic practice, the divine feminine, and spiritualism. This can make her a challenging card for readers and querents (myself included) who have a secular relationship with the tarot. The thing to remember is you don't actually need to know *how* she does what she does in order to believe in her magic. The High Priestess' power, by another name, is intuition. Regardless of whether you believe that the explanation for why intuition can be uncannily accurate is scientific or supernatural, you can still remain open to it.

The High Priestess is about those times when you listen to your gut. We're not talking about superstitions and premonitions – just times when you have a strong sense about a person or a situation. You know the feeling when you meet someone and, within a few words, are sure they're going to be part of your life? That's a High Priestess moment. Those times when you can't shake the sense – even though they haven't said anything, even though it feels a little silly – that someone you know isn't OK, and that you need to check on them and let them know you love them? That's her too. Those times when something doesn't feel right and you know you need to leave, or do something, or speak out? High Priestess again. The High Priestess is in the good vibes, the bad ones, and the weird ones. She encourages you to acknowledge them and to explore what they mean.

She's not, however, giving you permission to allow your intuition to run amok. Sometimes, when we tamp down our instincts and ignore subtle signs that something isn't right, it ends badly. There have been times in my life when I've met someone and, within the space of our first conversation, found myself feeling like a cat whose fur has been brushed backwards: a profound conviction that I just don't like this person. Often, I've pushed through the feeling... only to have my instinct proven correct, sometimes quietly, sometimes dramatically. (It hasn't always ended with me screaming, 'IF I NEVER SEE YOU AGAIN, IT'LL STILL BE TOO SOON', but I would be lying if I said that's never happened.) But there are also times when first impressions are misleading, or when someone doesn't realise that what they're experiencing isn't intuitive wisdom, it's unconscious bias. This card is about tempering the rational mind, not about overthrowing it.

This, really, is the gift of The High Priestess. She's an invitation to reclaim the irrational: to realise that it's not always a dirty word. We are not creatures who think and behave with perfect logic, and that's as it should be. Irrationality is part of us. It's in the instincts honed by a thousand generations. Irrationality is the home of our intuition. When we accept this aspect of ourselves, when we recognise that there are times when it should be embraced, we are, more often than not, rewarded for it. And maybe, just maybe, we open the door to magic – even if only of the smallest order.

QUESTIONS TO ASK WHEN YOU SEE THIS CARD: Do you know how to listen to your intuition? When do you let yourself be led by your gut? Are you ever too attached to being rational and logical? Can you allow things to be unexplainable, but true?

THE EMPRESS (III)

The Empress is usually depicted as a lovely ripe fruit of a woman: often in repose, heavily pregnant, and wearing a robe embroidered with pomegranates. Her presence has weight and gravity: she is of the earth, bound to it, and greatly pleased by it. She is languorous and beautiful and radiates fecundity and richness. And, when she appears, she invites you to think about nurture: about the things you care for until they ripen into lusciousness.

Exactly what those are is for a querent to decide. We all find different things that we want to cultivate: it might be a skill or a passion, relationships or friendships. It could be your own body, your art, your work, your mind. It could be a child – though it should go without saying that The Empress' pregnancy is metaphorical rather than literal. Her gift is in the act of creation: of pouring abundant energy and care into her charge, feeding it, watching it take shape. She knows that things grown with love bloom the brightest. She knows that it is impossible to be spoiled by goodness – only by coldness and withholding. The Empress reminds us never to starve the things that we care about.

The other important thing that she knows is how to wait. The Empress is very, very good at waiting. She knows that all things have a season, that they come when they're ready, and, if you rush them, they often emerge as pale shadows of what they could have been, flimsy and fragile and not yet strong enough to withstand the blows of the world. Sometimes, we try to push ourselves into actions that we aren't really prepared for, or try to force a connection that hasn't had enough time to take root. Sometimes we get frustrated with ourselves or with others when something we want doesn't seem to be happening quickly enough. The Empress asks you to consider whether that's a fair and accurate assessment of the situation. Perhaps there *is* movement, and it's just that it's slow. Perhaps it's winding up into motion – invisible to the naked eye, but no less real because of that.

Quite often when people turn to the tarot, the last thing they want is to be told to have patience. As a society, we've grown accustomed to immediacy. We can buy anything we want, right now, with next-day delivery, even if we don't have the money for it. Whatever question we ask, the internet will have the answer in a matter of seconds. And there's always someone, somewhere, sharing easy tips to help us achieve our goals in no time at all. The Empress represents the opposite of that lifestyle. She tells us that when we have to put time and effort into creating something, we value the fruits of our labours all the more (this, apparently, is why people are so fond of IKEA furniture).

One of the lovely things about sitting patiently, as The Empress does, is that you get to watch. You get to notice all of the tiny details of passing time: the budding and blossoming, the flight of birds, the clouds sailing by. You might discover something you'd have missed by rushing. Good things come to those who wait – but they can come while you wait, too.

QUESTIONS TO ASK WHEN YOU SEE THIS CARD: What are you cultivating or nurturing in your life? Are you trying to rush something, someone, or yourself? Is there something that seems to be taking a painfully long time? Can you be alright with needing to wait?

THE EMPEROR (IV)

The Emperor is a card which, for a modern-day tarot reader, can be difficult. In fairly stark contrast to when the tarot was invented, empires and emperors are – rightly – no longer considered to be good things. And this card is almost always depicted as a masculine figure of authority: literally a patriarch.

There are plenty of times, therefore, when his appearance prompts necessary conversations about decolonisation, dismantling the patriarchy, or relationships with paternal authority figures – particularly difficult, overbearing ones. If that's what comes up most strongly when a querent sees him, explore it – this card can and does create a safe space to talk about some difficult topics. Those old systems have had profoundly damaging and far-reaching effects on generations of human beings. And their figureheads – the people who hold traditional positions of authority – are distrusted for a reason. Emperors are synonymous with oppression, with failing their subjects, often repeatedly and sometimes in profoundly cruel and violent ways. The shadow side of this card is exactly what you'd expect: it can represent aspects of structures and the self that are rigid, dictatorial, and unfeeling. It can represent those who do not deserve their crowns, and ought to be toppled from their thrones.

But don't let that be the limit of your understanding of this card. The Emperor also speaks to the ways in which you can benefit from authority, and confer its benefits upon others. Authority, in this case, does not mean patriarchal authority: something conferred by status, birth, or identity. It means leadership that is earned through compassion and trust. The Emperor can refer to aspects of the self that are worth striving for: the ability to take responsibility and, in doing so, to create positive change and situations for the people around you. Being direct, knowing how to be accountable for your actions, and using your knowledge and experience to serve others is far from a bad thing.

There is a line in Lauren Groff's novel *Matrix* which I think neatly sums up what sits at the heart of The Emperor's gift: 'It is a deep and human truth that most souls upon the earth are not at ease unless they find themselves safe in a force far greater than themselves.' Crucially, this quote describes the reaction of a group of people to a magnificent twelfth-century nun who almost single-handedly restores the workings and fortunes of a failing abbey and the community that surrounds it. The Emperor is not The Man or even, necessarily, A Man. It's anyone or anything that offers protection or direction when you need it. At its best, it's something to which you submit with relief: a doctor's coat, a pilot's licence, a steady, calm voice when you're panicking, even just 'mind the gap' on a train platform. The Emperor represents individual leaders and figures of authority, but also: seatbelts.

The Emperor is a weighty card, and one that has picked up difficult semiotic associations over time – so if he causes discomfort in a reading, don't ignore it. But it's also one of the places in the tarot where your knowledge of the card's deeper symbolism is most valuable for a querent. The Emperor can be benevolent – the symbol of forces and people that shelter us and protect us, and under whose wings we feel safe. It is always worth exploring both sides of his coin.

QUESTIONS TO ASK WHEN YOU SEE THIS CARD: What or who does this card bring up for you, and how do you feel about it? Where do you find your safety and protection? How do you show leadership to others? What is your relationship with authority?

THE HIEROPHANT (V)

HIERARCHIES, SYSTEMS, RULES, POWER STRUGGLES, HIGHER
SELVES, BREAKING WITH TRADITION

The Hierophant is a prime example of the tarot being created
in a dim and distant past, when someone might have seen an
image of the Pope on his Pope-throne and thought, 'Yes, this
reflects my state of mind right now – oh, how well this card
captures the essence of my daily challenges.' Nowadays, it's
somewhat less likely to resonate at first glance (unless, maybe,
you are the Pope?).

For a modern-day audience and for the purposes of a tarot
reading, it is helpful to know that a hierophant is a person,
especially a priest, who interprets sacred mysteries or esoteric

principles. And what are our modern-day sacred mysteries and esoteric principles if not the systems and powers that govern and control our lives? The Hierophant is an embodiment of the organisations and institutions that surround us, from businesses to academia, government to the legal system. He is, in a word, society – the rules (written or otherwise) which we collectively uphold, and which we are all expected to observe in order to remain part of the group.

The role of The Hierophant, then, is that of teacher and mentor. He explains the rules and helps you to follow them. It's worth noting that the Hierophant is the masculine counterpoint to the High Priestess, but where she is tapped into the subtleties of her intuition, his approach is rather more practical – he's all about applied learning. In that sense, he represents the resources that you have at your disposal to do whatever it is you're trying to do. If you're preparing for an exam or trying to hit targets for a promotion, The Hierophant represents the materials and the work of studying: the books, the memory exercises, the effort. He can also represent an ally – the good manager with a worksheet on your assessment objectives and a plan for how you'll meet them. This card speaks to the fact that almost anything can be learnt, and that there is almost always someone or something who can teach you the way.

Of course, the other thing about rules – and, indeed, about Rome – is that you need to know when to break with them. The Hierophant is a reminder that understanding the status quo is a prerequisite for challenging it. And this is where the card's shadow side dwells. He's used to being in charge – someone made him the head of the church and the gateway to all these sacred mysteries and he'll be damned if he's giving that up. So if you're trying to break with tradition, shatter a glass ceiling, or even just chat to your grandad about politics, you may find yourself up against a great deal of resistance. The hardest part of encountering The Hierophant is knowing whether you should work with him, push against him, or throw him in the bin.

This card represents decisions about whether or not you're going to obey the rules. It can offer structure and support on the journey, teaching you what you need to know to achieve your goals. But it's also important to be able to recognise when the lesson is over, when you no longer need that external validation, and it's time to deviate from tradition.

QUESTIONS TO ASK WHEN YOU SEE THIS CARD: What are you working on? What do you need to know or learn to achieve a goal? Where do you find mentorship and teaching? Do you feel that you know enough? Are you ready to go your own way?

THE LOVERS (VI)

COMMITMENT, HARMONY, EQUALITY, BONDING, INTENSITY,
OBSESSION, IMBALANCE

You have met The Lovers before. It's that new couple who can't
keep their gazes (or hands) off one another, who feel that they
have found their soulmate. They are recognisable protagonists
in certain genres of fiction: the great loves that overcome
every barrier to be together. Perhaps they talk about being
twin flames: the Platonic idea that each person carries half a
soul, and can only truly be fulfilled when they find the other
half and become pair-bonded again, united within the greater
entity of 'us'.

Depending on where you're standing, this kind of rhetoric

can seem desperately romantic and wonderful, insufferably smug, slightly ridiculous, or even somewhat problematic. That's kind of the point of The Lovers, and why you should be very wary of taking it at face value when you encounter it. This card is not here to tell you that you have a relationship without flaws, or that yours is a love story for all the ages. It's a card that reminds you that after infatuation has burnt away, you have a choice: to stay or to go. It's a card that holds up any ideal – not just a romantic ideal – and asks how you're feeling about it right now. Generally, the answer is: it's complicated.

The Lovers has a significant shadow side, which I like to call The Full Enrique, in honour of Enrique Iglesias's song *Escape*, whose narrator invites the object of his affections to run and hide from him while noting that they will not be able to outrun his overpowering feelings. This is a weird dynamic, but also a familiar one. Most people know what it's like to be in the first flushes of love. Those early days are the stuff of love songs: you would do anything; your love will conquer all; it's you and me against the world, etc. But the thing about love songs is that they're terrible at showing you what a healthy relationship should look like. The Lovers says that finding someone about whom you feel so strongly is a fabulous starting point, but maybe don't expect that to be enough on its own. It can open up conversations about what you expect from relationships, specifically, whether you might be waiting for an idealised, epic fantasy version of love that perhaps doesn't exist.

This card is far from a negative one, though – even in its shadow side, it's mostly a reality check. It's rare that a querent isn't excited or at least a little intrigued when this card appears in a reading. But The Lovers doesn't *have* to refer to romantic pairs. In fact, its most beautiful showings tend not to speak to relationships with other people at all. The Lovers' gift is harmony, commitment, and a bond that can weather any storm. And perhaps you don't have to look beyond yourself to find that.

The Lovers can ask you: what if you could achieve harmony by loving and respecting yourself? What if your partner (if you have one) could be just that: a beloved companion along the way, but still an individual in their own right? There is something strange, I think, in the idea of the 'other half', implying as it does that we are all fundamentally lacking. The Lovers, at its best, asks you to look inwards, to see yourself as complete, as yin and yang, as question and answer, all within the one soul. It says you don't have to have gaps to fill – only love to give.

QUESTIONS TO ASK WHEN YOU SEE THIS CARD: How do you envisage love? Do you believe in perfect soulmates? How does that play out in your romantic life? How do you feel about yourself? Do you believe that you're enough? Do you love yourself?

THE CHARIOT (VII)

SUCCESS, FOCUS, OBSESSION, DETERMINATION, SPEED, OBSTINACY,
RECKLESSNESS, DISTRACTION, LOSS OF CONTROL

'At dawn, we ride,' says The Chariot. And wow, do we ever. Sometimes in life, you need to be reminded of your own power: to believe that you are the narrator of your own story; that you are not buffeted around by the whims of fortune, but can saddle your destiny and, as a former colleague was wont to say, 'Ride it – ride it like Seabiscuit!' (ie: to victory). This is the card of absolute obsessive focus on a goal, and of throwing all of your energy into achieving it. Full steam ahead, says The Chariot. Wherever you're going, you're going there FAST.

A word of caution before you crack the whip and push those

horses to a gallop, though. The symbolism of charioteering does raise a couple of red flags that are worth your attention. Firstly, chariots tend to be used in races and in wars, which means that this is not a fun run: you may be met with anything from resistance to outright opposition along the way (most chariot-drivers wore armour for exactly that reason). Second, chariots also tend to lack safety features and – given that you're meant to go pretty fast in them – that can be an issue. You'll need to hold on tight (know your goal!), keep your focus on the road ahead, and be prepared to navigate obstacles – whether that's with impressive evasive driving or just, you know, running them over. Courage, confidence, and a determination that unites both heart and mind are required to pilot The Chariot.

When it's good, it is very, very good. The Chariot doesn't just speak to determination and direction for yourself – it can be a powerful influence on others. It can involve going against the grain and the status quo, and being the one who leads the way to something new. Watch a shoal of fish or a murmuration of starlings and you'll quickly see how one creature changing its trajectory is enough to shift the course of the whole group. You could be that bird, or that mackerel! The fact that the road you've chosen isn't the one that everyone else is on is a challenge, but not an insurmountable one. Even if it feels like everything is set against you, willpower and determination can prevail.

When it's bad, though, The Chariot is disastrous. The shadow side of this card isn't hard to guess at. Rather than a splendid charge towards sure triumph, it's more... Mr Toad's wild ride in *The Wind in the Willows*. It's a reckless amphibian with little talent for driving and no sense of direction, who has somehow commandeered a motorcar, and is about to endanger lives and cause major damage to property. In other words, it's absolutely terrifying, and likely to result in the fast-moving

vehicle being found upended in a ditch. If that feels familiar –
if your chariot is careening out of control – take notice. This
could be your opportunity to re-evaluate whether you really
ought to be driving at 110mph (short answer: no). Sometimes
when things aren't working out, we need to refocus our attention. Sometimes we need to go in with greater conviction. And
sometimes, we need to stop.

QUESTIONS TO ASK WHEN YOU SEE THIS CARD: What's your objective? Do you believe in it, even if others don't? Are you ready to
make a run for it? What obstacles do you face along the way
and how will you navigate them? How's the journey going? Are
you sure you know what you're doing? Wait, did you even pass
your driving test?

STRENGTH (VIII)

SELF-KNOWLEDGE, RESTRAINT, ACCEPTANCE, HUMILITY, GRACE,
ENDURANCE, COMPOSURE, DOUBT, PRIMAL INSTINCT

Strength isn't about physical, brute strength – this is not a tarot card that indicates you are, or need to become, very muscular. Instead, it speaks to something quieter and more introspective: fortitude, the strength that comes from within, from truly knowing, accepting, and trusting yourself. And, though it might not be a dramatic act, it nevertheless takes courage. In most decks, Strength is depicted as a young woman prying open the jaws of a lion, with much the same expression as a dog owner whose pet has just grabbed a chicken bone off the pavement. Her face is calm – maybe even a little weary. The beast tends not to look delighted, but it's not snarling, either. This isn't a battle or a circus trick. There's a sense of mutual respect and co-operation. The woman isn't controlling the creature, nor is the creature controlling her.

When Strength appears in a reading, you're being offered a chance to think about how you handle yourself. Where does your inner strength come from and how does it manifest in your life? Are you able to sit with discomfort? Are you at the mercy of your feelings or can you rise above them? When criticised, are you able to quell the urge to attack or defend, and find stillness and wisdom before you respond? We all have passionate and primal instincts, and there are times when they serve us well. But there are also times when the reptilian brain, the part of us that is prepared to do anything to survive, needs to be wrestled with. There are moments when we get to decide to do things differently.

This is the card that asks us to make friends with all of the wild, untamed, untidy, and unnamed parts of ourselves, the parts that we might have denied, ignored, or have been taught to repress. In King Khan's Black Power Tarot, Strength is portrayed by the singer Tina Turner. Originally King Khan planned to depict Turner wrestling with her alleged former abuser, but the filmmaker and tarot reader Alejandro Jodorowsky, Khan's mentor, advised him to keep the traditional lion in the card. To do anything else would be to fundamentally misunderstand its meaning. Strength isn't about how we approach the outside world: it is about how we face ourselves.

For me, it's impossible to look at Strength and not think of the ways in which feminist writers have played with the age-old Beauty and the Beast tale: transforming it from a story about masculine aggression being soothed by feminine gentleness into an allegory about uniting aspects of oneself. The Beast is revealed to be not an intruder or a threat, but an aspect of the Beauty that she's previously stifled for being too wild, too sensual. When he appears, as Marina Warner writes in *From The Beast To The Blonde*, the Beast 'holds up a mirror to the force of nature within her, which she is invited to accept and to allow to grow.' Sometimes, Strength asks a querent to consider whether there are parts of themself that have been smothered. It's a reminder that repressing your wildness isn't the same as understanding it; that true strength lies in self-knowledge and in radical self-acceptance.

QUESTIONS TO ASK WHEN YOU SEE THIS CARD: Do you know and embrace your whole self? Are you tapped into your more primal urges, or do you repress them? Are you ruled by your instincts, or have you mastered them? Do they ever lead you into danger?

THE HERMIT (IX)

The Hermit usually provokes an immediate reaction from querents when it appears: they either love it or they hate it. People who see themselves in this card tend to be introverts who gather their energy from within. Those who reject it lean towards extroversion. Needless to say, the latter group often needs a bit more persuasion in order to accept what The Hermit has to offer.

First and foremost, it's important to note that The Hermit is not about exclusion. Not at all. Historically, hermits weren't ostracised – they were people who retreated into solitude for various purposes, but who were supported by their communities, or at least treated with respect. When this card appears in a reading, it's not about people not wanting to spend time with you: it's about you not wanting to spend time with other people. It's an acknowledgement of the restorative power of turning your gaze inwards and choosing solitude. In most decks, The Hermit holds aloft a lantern in which a tiny star is burning, reminding you that sometimes you can become so focused on chasing the brightness and dazzle of others that you forget your own light. It's an invitation to retreat within your shell for a moment, to sit with your thoughts and feelings, to notice and be nourished by them. The world will still be there for you when you're ready to come back.

For me, The Hermit always recalls a time when, after one of the worst years of my life (so far!), I decided to spend a week on my own in the Scottish Highlands. This was just as autumn turned to winter, and my accommodation was a shepherd's hut with no electricity or running water. I walked a lot, read a lot, chopped and burnt a lot of logs, and spoke to absolutely no one who wasn't a sheep. It was – and I cannot stress this enough – amazing. Somehow, that week alone, spent immersed in nature and in my own thoughts, helped me to begin the difficult work of piecing together a new sense of myself from the fragmented ruins of the old.

One of the things I read that week was a book of poetry, *In the Cairngorms*, by Nan Shepherd, a woman who lived most of her life alone in the same tiny Cairngorms cottage. She writes about wild places as a space for deconstructing yourself into your rawest component parts, and then beginning again: 'Now she may recreate herself. / Now is the primal day.' Like a butterfly's chrysalis, The Hermit can offer more than just restoration and recuperation: it can be a site of transformation.

And, just like a chrysalis, it's not meant to be a permanent state of being. That's the shadow in this card: sometimes, when you stay away for too long, the transition back can be painful. You can get stuck in your cocoon, or resist re-emerging. It's always worth pointing out that The Hermit isn't meant to be forever: it's about carving out a window of solitude that's the right size for your needs. And it's a reminder that one of the greatest joys of time spent alone is the moment of returning to the world – grounded, restored, even renewed – and seeing it differently.

QUESTIONS TO ASK WHEN YOU SEE THIS CARD: Do you feel comfortable being on your own? Do you give yourself enough time to be alone? Do you ever give yourself too much? Do you feel guilty about stepping back from others? Do you trust people to still be there when you return?

WHEEL OF FORTUNE (X)

UNPREDICTABILITY, UNCERTAINTY, THE UNEXPECTED,
CIRCUMSTANCE, FATE, COINCIDENCE, INSTABILITY, FEAR

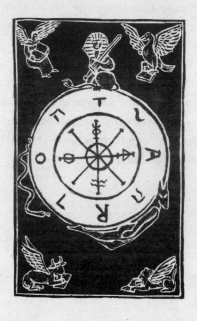

The Wheel of Fortune is the tarot's reminder of the unpredictable nature of life. Change, as they say, is our only constant. This card tells us that you might wake up and, with no warning, discover that today is a day you'll never forget. Or you might wake up and find it's… just another day. It is also, essentially, the tarot's disclaimer. Because if you're asking the tarot a question (Am I going to meet the love of my life this year? Will I change jobs? Is it going to rain?) and this card appears, you need to take it for what it is: a hands-up admission that the tarot cannot see everything that is coming your way. By all means, exercise your free will! But also be prepared for fate, chance, the universe, or whatever else you want to call it to intervene at random. You can't pin down the future. Sorry. No refunds.

But, asks The Wheel of Fortune, would you really want spoilers anyway? Sarah Moss' novel *The Tidal Zone* wrestles with that question: whether knowing exactly what was going to happen to you and your loved ones – not just the good stuff but also the bad, 'their loves and losses, triumphs and failures, sicknesses and last moments' – would actually be such a good thing. Probably not, is the conclusion: 'You think you want a story, you think you want an ending, but you don't. You want life. You want disorder and ignorance and uncertainty.' That's one of the painful things about the condition of being alive, but it's also the source of some of its greatest joys. If you knew everything that was going to happen to you, it would spoil those transcendent moments that you had no idea were coming. (And if they had advance warning of the less good bits, most people would probably fall apart before they even left the house.)

So when The Wheel of Fortune comes up, try to see it for its gift: an invitation to live with and embrace change, and to explore new opportunities as they arise, even – or especially – if they weren't what you were expecting. It's a moment to ask yourself how you deal with uncertainty. Can you live with it, and within it? It can also prompt conversations about the techniques you use to help yourself feel in control in an unpredictable world. Do you have coping mechanisms that help to ground you and give you comfort? Are they healthy and constructive, or do they hold you back?

The other lesson of The Wheel of Fortune is that, if change is constant... then change is constant. Nothing stays the same forever, not even bad things. If this card appears for you at a time when things are tough and challenging, it can be a reminder of the power of just hunkering down, and doing whatever you need to get by until the disturbance passes. It's no coincidence that often this card is depicted as a compass or the wheel of a ship: you don't have to be an experienced sailor to know that travelling by boat means that you're at the mercy of some very powerful elements. Sometimes, when a storm races through your life, you must bend so that you don't break. Sometimes, you just have to wait it out.

QUESTIONS TO ASK WHEN YOU SEE THIS CARD: Where in your life do you feel uncertainty? How does the future make you feel? Do you have reliable coping mechanisms? Are you flexible enough to withstand the unexpected? Do you know how to wait out a storm?

JUSTICE (XI)

INEVITABILITY, ACCOUNTABILITY, FATE, ACCEPTANCE, RESOLUTION,
DISPASSIONATE ACTIONS, LAW, BALANCE, DISCOMFORT, TRUTH

You might assume, when you see the Justice card, that it means
that justice is about to be served, and that you are about to
be vindicated. You would be wrong. While there are some
situations where that interpretation might make sense or feel
reassuring, it's not the point at all. Justice promises a decision,
but not necessarily a favourable one. It's blind, it's implacable,
it follows the law, and it is, without a doubt, problematic.

Many people rightly struggle with the coldness of this card
and its overt associations with the legal system. It's all very well
to announce that you're going to strip away emotions, feelings,

and philosophy, and act upon laws, precedents, and codes. But who's to say that those codes aren't flawed. Where do they originate? To whom do they belong and who do they benefit? Whose 'objective' truth do they represent? The world is not a level playing field and, regardless of the theory, in practice, some people seem to be better at getting 'justice' than others. This card promises truth, but it's hard to avoid bias.

Balances and imbalances of power are at the heart of Justice, and when it comes up in a reading, that's worth exploring. When I see it, I can't help but think of a page in a lo-fi, celebrity-themed Powerpoint that a friend sent to me after I lost my job a few years ago. Across a tabloid photograph of some Chihuahuas she wrote, in large Comic Sans, 'If the pained expressions of Paris Hilton's pets can teach us anything, it is that the wrong people are sometimes in charge of our fate.' Obviously, it was hilarious, which I needed, but it stuck with me (and has been shared with many people in need of support since) because it so perfectly captured the baffling bizarreness of my situation. There are moments when someone or something uses their power to screw you over and, no matter how unfair, no matter how articulate your objections, nothing will change it. Justice can and should prompt conversations about the times when we experience injustices, whether great or petty ones. Indeed, this is one of the cards in the tarot whose shadow often seems to be dominant.

It took me a long time to find the other side of Justice – the gift, such as it is. In the end, what revealed it was thinking about a different kind of law: the sort that no one living or dead had a hand in making. In the Nomad Tarot, Justice is depicted as a fox with a bird in its jaws and the deck's creator, Jennifer Dranttel, writes that it 'speaks to the immutable laws of the universe.' Nature isn't cold or cruel or unjust: it just *is*. When you watch a wildlife documentary, you root for predator or prey depending on the angle of the edit, but neither is actually a hero or a villain. You might not have enjoyed physics at school but you also can't really protest against Newton's laws of motion. Sometimes, Justice says, things just happen. And then the balance rights itself. And then the cycle goes on.

Justice can speak not only to the codes we create for ourselves, but to the vast and unknowable laws of the cosmos. When it appears, it's a chance to ask if you can accept what's happening – and, sometimes, whether you should.

QUESTIONS TO ASK WHEN YOU SEE THIS CARD: Are you stuck on anything right now? Do you feel wronged? Is holding on to that feeling helpful? Is there anything that you can do about it? Can you accept it?

THE HANGED MAN (XII)

SACRIFICE, RELEASE, SUBMISSION, NEW PERSPECTIVE, LIMINALITY,
ACCEPTANCE, PAUSING, LIMBO, INDECISION

'Ankle' is the first and most important word to say here. The Hanged Man is hanged by his ankle, and not by his neck. He is not dead or dying or being punished. He is in a pose of submission, dangling upside down from a tree, between the sky and the earth, in order to undergo a transformation. I don't think it's a coincidence that his head-down position is similar to that of a baby getting ready to be born. He seeks a new way of being, and the cost of finding it is his comfort.

The lesson of The Hanged Man exists in various idioms, both lofty and prosaic. It's that the price of knowledge is sacrifice; that you can't have your cake and eat it too; that there's no such thing as a free lunch. The Hanged Man reminds us that sometimes in order to move ahead you must let something else go. It's the sort of lesson we instinctively rail against: human beings do not like to lose things. In fact, we're more powerfully motivated by the risk of loss than we are by the potential for gain. We like to believe that if we can just hold things close enough, they'll stay unchanged forever. Often, The Hanged Man's arrival challenges that comforting, but ultimately false, belief.

And sometimes when it appears, this card is an invitation to consider things that you've been afraid to look at too closely. Those dreams, desires, or wishes, or possible future versions of yourself that you avoid contemplating, because to chase after them would be to throw away everything you've won, built, or amassed thus far. It would mean dismantling what you know of the world, or of yourself – and that cost is too high, isn't it? (Or is it?) Sometimes, those are the feelings and thoughts to which this card demands the most careful attention be paid.

In Kathleen Jamie's beautiful poem, 'The Hinds', the narrator watches a herd of deer streaming through a glen before they pause to gaze back at her. In its final lines, she imagines their matriarch as a fairy queen beckoning her into another realm: '*Aren't we / the bonniest companie? / Come to me, / you'll be happy but never go home.*' The poem prickles my senses in the same way The Hanged Man does. It poses an almost impossible question: how great a sacrifice are you willing to make? Will you hold fast to the security of the known, or could you let it go to find something greater? And how would you live with the ache of knowing that, whichever you choose, the other is lost?

The Hanged Man's truth isn't an easy one, but it's offered up gently. The card shows you what you need to do to move forwards, but it doesn't – cannot – force you into action. Sometimes, it prompts conversations about feeling stuck or knowing that there's a difficult decision ahead that you're not ready to make. Remember that it's alright to stay in that place for a while, if that's what you need. The Hanged Man knows that it can take time to reorient your perspective on the world, to grow into your new knowledge, your new self. This is a between-space, a liminal space, and you can only cross it once you're ready.

QUESTIONS TO ASK WHEN YOU SEE THIS CARD: What have you been holding on to, and is it time to let go? Do you feel ready to make a sacrifice? Do you feel as though you are living between two realities? Are you stuck, or can you be released?

DEATH (XIII)

ENDINGS, TRANSFORMATION, CHANGE, NEW BEGINNINGS,
CLOSURE, FEAR, RELAPSE

In the tarot, Death does not necessarily – or even usually – mean
death. It's easy to see why people might think it does, what with
the name and also the image on the Rider Waite Smith card of
the Grim Reaper riding across a field of dead and dying bodies.
But please allow me to reassure you that the Death card does
not mean someone's about to die.

That said, it's not exactly an easy ride. When you see
the Death card, you're being asked to think about endings: the
ones that close chapters and complete cycles. Relationships,
jobs, houses, the end of a decade in your life – it can speak to

any of those things and more, some of them more difficult than others. It's also worth noting that, while this card doesn't predict death, death does happen to everyone, and its appearance in a reading can create space for people to reflect on their own experiences of loss. The Death card can and should open up conversations about how we experience endings of all sorts. It's also a reminder that death is part of the circle of life. When something dies, it leads to new growth: metaphorical rebirth. The atoms that make up our bodies were all a thousand other things before they were us, and who knows what they will become in future?

The aspect of this card that people tend to struggle with isn't the possibility of transformation but the pain of ending; the work of bringing an old life, an old version of you, old ways of being and thinking and feeling, to a close; and, most of all, the act of saying goodbye. When the Death card arrives in a reading, the question that most people find themselves asking is, *Am I ready for this?* Sometimes, the answer is no. But crucially (and this is where this card differs from its predecessor, The Hanged Man), when Death is around, the answer being 'no' doesn't make any difference. This card speaks to the times when, even if you're not ready, even if every fibre of your being wants to hold on, the change – the end – is coming for you. Death, metaphorical or otherwise, is inevitable. The gift and the challenge of Death is accepting it. When that's possible, it can liberate you. And when it's not, it can feel more like an act of vandalism. The tarot might not have an answer to that feeling but, if it's a familiar one, perhaps this card is a chance to sit with it for a moment.

The idea of Death is that it is a one-way journey. Often it is. But sometimes, you can still go back to pick over the bones or invite the ghosts of the past to haunt you. And that's where this card's shadow lies: relapsing into old patterns and old habits, forgetting that they ended for a reason. There are times when the Death card asks you to truly square up to whatever it is that you need to part with in your life so that you don't go down that path. Closing a door is one thing. Locking it is another.

QUESTIONS TO ASK WHEN YOU SEE THIS CARD: Are you facing, or have you recently experienced, an ending in some part of your life? Are you resisting change? Is there something that no longer serves you? Are you revisiting things that ought to be left to lie? What does this ending potentially open up in your future? What new thing would you like to bring into your life next?

TEMPERANCE (XIV)

BALANCE, MODERATION, CONTROL, ALCHEMY, EXCESS,
EXTREMES, IMBALANCE

When you start out with the tarot, there are some cards that immediately speak to you, and others whose appearance you dread. Temperance is, for many people (myself included), that card.

It makes sense, really, because Temperance is the card of balance and moderation and, for most of the people I know, that's not familiar territory. A healthy medium is not the default condition of modern living. Our culture pushes us towards productivity and excess: we are repeatedly told we can do more and achieve more, work harder, jump higher, consume better, and optimise ourselves to achieve the dream. As the eponymous lead of the sitcom *Frasier* once said: 'If less is more, think how much more more could be.' As the saying goes, 'Everything in moderation, including moderation.' Temperance is emphatically *not* about that life.

The good news about this card is that it's not here to grill you about your exercise, diet, alcohol consumption, credit card use, or sleeping habits. The bad news is that it's asking for you to achieve something trickier. Moderation is often figured as offsetting bad behaviours with good ones, but Temperance doesn't believe that you can counterbalance your way out of trouble. It asks for nothing less than alchemy: the ability to gracefully blend different or opposing forces into something new and far superior. In the Rider Waite Smith, this is depicted as an angel who defies gravity to make liquid flow upwards from one cup to another. In the Wild Unknown deck, it's a heron which melds flame and water together. Temperance represents something that isn't easy or spontaneous. It speaks to a skill or a practice that requires you to expertly control volatile and often totally conflicting elements. Is that something you recognise? Or is it something you seek?

When Temperance appears in a reading, it's an invitation to think about where and if you have that kind of control in your life. It's not telling you to give everything up and become a monk, but it might prompt conversations about whether you have a clear vision and a steady path, or whether it feels more like you're constantly lurching between extremes, trying to fight fires and compensate for things you have or haven't done. Sometimes, it can be a prompt to stop, take a breath, and collect yourself, rather than continue living like you're in a pinball machine.

Temperance also underscores the importance of being aware of the impact that both your expectations of yourself, and those of others, can have on you. To live is to change: sometimes naturally and of your own accord, and sometimes in response to other people's urgings. This card can be a reminder that there's a fine balance between being adaptable and open to growth, and being so malleable that you end up sacrificing yourself on the altar of other people's opinions. You cannot be all things to all people: being a chameleon is an art, but it's also a drain on your energy. This card can ask if you're wearing too many masks, or flitting through too many selves in order to please others. Perhaps it's time to drop the grand gestures and quick costume changes and instead draw on the gifts this card offers: patience, care, and authenticity.

QUESTIONS TO ASK WHEN YOU SEE THIS CARD: What does your life look like today? Where is there balance and where is there imbalance? What does the word moderation mean to you? What challenges do you face? Are you true to yourself, or are you heavily influenced by others?

THE DEVIL (XV)

PATTERNS, CYCLES, DEFENSIVENESS, ADDICTION, SELF-LIMITING
BELIEFS, CONTROL, LIBERATION

Oh, hello there. It's the Devil. He might not be your favourite card, but please don't write him off – there's more to him than what you see on the surface. Is he actually Satan? No. Does he have some big questions for you to ask yourself? Yes, of course he does. This Devil is the lord of patterns, of circles and cycles that go round and round and round and round. And when he appears, it's time to ask yourself whether you're spiralling upwards or downwards.

You probably intuitively know what he means in his most direct interpretation: he's the ultimate shadow side in the tarot.

He can speak to some of the most significant manifestations of negative forces in life: self-destructive patterns of behaviour, addictions, toxic relationships. If those don't feel like familiar places, you might recognise him in his less dramatic, but not always less damaging, incarnations: really, any cycle of behaviour by which you can be entrapped. Some are true vices and difficult feelings – fear, anger, self-loathing – while others might feel more like bad habits: ping-ponging in and out of your overdraft, constantly putting yourself down, or pushing your body to its limits rather than offering it care. The Devil even lives in some of the more prosaic cycles: the morning coffee that you just *have* to have in order to function, and the job you hate but won't leave because you're used to the lifestyle it affords you.

The challenge of this card is clear, but the gift isn't quite so obvious – you have to look closer to find it. In most depictions of The Devil, we see a horned beast with two figures on either side of him, chained by the neck. The chains are loose. Very loose. If they wanted to, The Devil's prisoners could lift them up and walk free. Similarly, in the Nomad Tarot, The Devil is represented as a spider's web, a labyrinthine construction of spirals and threads – but it's an empty one, with no predator sitting at its heart. The truth is that it's the pattern that's trapping you, not some unseen dictatorial authority. The Devil speaks to the times when, actually, it isn't entirely someone else's fault. It's a reminder that it's not always true when we tell ourselves that things can't change, that we're stuck like this, that it's beyond our control, that it is what it is. And that knowledge can be liberating. It can be the first step in doing things differently.

This card offers up a choice. There's the path of least resistance, of continuing the cycle and the pattern – or there's choosing to fight the tide. It goes without saying that the second option isn't likely to be easy. Old habits die hard, and it can take years of work and support to break the most destructive cycles. But it is possible – and maybe, just maybe, it's time. When The Devil appears, he's asking you if you are ready to confront those parts of your life and yourself. He's a reminder of your power to do so. He tells you that you might have to dig deep, and ask for help, and challenge your own assumptions about the world, but he also tells you that you can do it. You really can.

QUESTIONS TO ASK WHEN YOU SEE THIS CARD: What are the things that you feel trapped in, or from which you take comfort? What are the things that you believe you can't escape? Is that true? What are the patterns that you've witnessed over and over in your life? Are they helpful or are they harmful?

THE TOWER (XVI)

UNEXPECTED CHANGE, CATASTROPHE, REVELATION, DESTRUCTION,
REVOLUTION, TRANSFORMATION, TRUTH

The Tower is one of the most difficult cards in the deck. It represents a shocking, unexpected change when structures that had previously seemed solid and impregnable suddenly tumble down. It's an almighty shattering of the status quo, when truths are revealed to be hollow, when the rug is pulled from beneath your feet, or when the life you thought you were leading suddenly takes a very different direction. It can speak to some of the most difficult of all human experiences: bereavements, betrayals, losses, and changes that come out of nowhere and leave you reeling. It's about any event that shifts your foundations and throws your sense of self off balance.

If this card appears when you're reading for someone else, tread softly. There are very few people who, by the time they reach adulthood, haven't experienced a Tower moment, and this card can bring up difficult memories. Sometimes, the memories are fresh – sometimes, people are still standing in the wreckage and wondering what to do now. This is one of the moments where the tarot doesn't offer advice: its gift is simply that it allows that person's story to be heard, and opens a door for them to sit with their feelings, alone or with others, for a while.

But The Tower isn't all bad – far from it. Turning points and realisations after which lives are irrevocably changed are certainly shocking, but they can also be necessary, and even beneficial. Sometimes, *you* are the person who strikes something down. The Tower can represent the cleansing fire, the scouring away of detritus, the decision to break away from structures, institutions, and connections that no longer serve you, or which no longer serve a purpose to anyone at all. As Fiona so eloquently puts it: sometimes The Tower means BURN IT ALL! BURN IT TO THE GROUND! Sometimes you are done – finished, *fin*! – with something. Sometimes, destruction can be positive: in demolishing the old, you're preparing the ground for building anew.

This is the card of revolutions both big and small; it's the card of social and political movements that say: enough, this stops here; and also the card of jacking in the job you hate, ending the relationship that isn't working, and maybe moving to the other side of the world. Those revolutions and those destructions don't have to be physical: The Tower can also represent a moment of phenomenal courage and conviction, the act of seeking out the truth of something, and the relief that you feel when you find it, when you are able to be honest with yourself and the world.

Another thing that I've noticed with this card is that, when it appears, it doesn't always speak to something that's actually happening, but instead to what you fear could. Sometimes, you conjure the spectre of The Tower in your mind, even when it's nowhere to be seen. It can be representative of catastrophic thinking: worrying about the worst possible outcomes, being constantly on guard and hyper-vigilant to threats. This isn't helpful, and it doesn't even make those shocking moments easier to bear. The final lesson of The Tower is that you shouldn't live your life in its shadow. It comes for us all once in a while, for good or for ill, but it is always, by definition, unexpected.

QUESTIONS TO ASK WHEN YOU SEE THIS CARD: Has anything happened that has completely uprooted you recently? How do you process upheaval? Is there anything that you think needs to be destroyed in order for you to move forwards? What do you most fear? Will worrying about it change anything?

THE STAR (XVII)

HOPE, RENEWAL, BELIEF, HEALING, TRANSFORMATION, LOSS OF FAITH, DESPAIR

The Star is almost always the most beautiful card in any tarot deck. Usually, it is depicted as a nude figure, alone in the starlight, one foot on land and the other in a flowing stream. It is blue and gold, calm and quiet. It's a card that speaks in whispers, but one which holds a special place in many readers' hearts. The best way to understand its energy is to remember (or imagine) a clear night, and a wide sky seen from a place where there's no light other than the glimmer of the constellations above you. It's the feeling of realising that you are just a tiny fragment of consciousness in an unfathomably large universe – and also that you are a natural and entirely perfect part of it. It's a place of peace and serenity.

Like many of the most beautiful things, this card has more than a touch of melancholy to it. It represents renewal, and so it necessarily encompasses past difficulties: a loss, a betrayal, a deep sadness, an ending. It's a reminder that, even in the depths of despair, hope can still exist. The Star always makes me think of a letter from E. B. White to a man who wrote to him saying that he had lost faith in humanity (which is, coincidentally, a feeling that this card's shadow side represents). White's response was to acknowledge the pain, but not to be overwhelmed by it: 'As long as there is one upright man, as long as there is one compassionate woman, the contagion may spread and the scene is not desolate. Hope is the thing that is left to us, in a bad time.'

Holding on to hope, particularly in the wake of trauma, or in the face of overwhelming difficulty, can feel pointless. But The Star asks us to do it anyway. It doesn't try to pretend that everything is fine now; it doesn't negate the past, or promise that the future will be perfect. It isn't about fixing things, because you do not need to be fixed. Your experiences are part of who you are, and who you'll become. This card acknowledges what has happened and it offers space to reflect – and to heal, if you need it – speaking to the ability to find peace within yourself, even when the world is in chaos. It is related, numerologically, to the Eights of the Minor Arcana, and to Strength: cards which speak to self-knowledge, self-acceptance, and moments when you are able to look within yourself, draw upon your power, and move forwards.

Indeed, perhaps the most beautiful offering of The Star is a reminder of what lies on the other side of experience. As Rebecca Solnit writes in *A Field Guide to Getting Lost*, 'Leave the door open for the unknown, the door into the dark. That's where the most important things come from, where you yourself came from, and where you will go.' We can't possibly anticipate or prepare ourselves for all that will happen in our lives. We survive more than we think we can bear. The gift in that, and the gift of The Star, is that we are transformed.

QUESTIONS TO ASK WHEN YOU SEE THIS CARD: What have you learnt along the way in your life? Have there been moments of sadness and pain that made you who you are? Would you do it all again? Are you able to face the unknown? Are you able to hold on to hope?

THE MOON (XVIII)

When you see The Moon (card) you'll probably think of the moon (celestial body), and that's not a bad place to start. There are a lot of questions to be asked about the moon, and about her relationship with human behaviour. Is she a soft and silvery watcher who keeps our secrets, or a spotlight that reveals things in too-stark detail? Is she our benevolent line manager in the sky, or a maddening force to whose will we are constantly bent?

'O moon / carrying inside yourself / your own death's head, your dark one / why do you chop yourself away / piece by piece,' asks Alice Oswald. The problem, and the point, is that the moon (celestial body) never answers. She rises and falls, fattens and dwindles, glows and fades. She is self-contained and reliably inconstant. The Moon (card) is exactly the same. When it appears it is, basically, an invitation for disorder. It tells us to forget the programme – we're past the part where there's a structure, and no one is in charge any more. Also all of the fact-checkers have been fired. The floor is open and we're now welcoming any and all contributions from our old friend: the subconscious.

This isn't the first time we've encountered the subconscious mind in the Majors. But, whereas The High Priestess represents channelling it into the tool of intuition, The Moon serves it up undiluted, pure, raw, and wild. It represents the feeling of being half-awake or feverish, when the real and the illusory collide and become indistinguishable from one another. It's the feeling of not being sure if you dreamt something, or if it really happened. It is grasping around in the dark, feeling entirely uncertain of your whereabouts. It asks, are you comfortable in these shadows or do you need to turn towards the light?

It is impossible to ignore the fact that this card can speak to mental illness, and to the slow decline of the mind that so many experience in later life. It can also be about times when old memories are dredged up like shipwrecks, and when you must reckon with the experiences that have shaped who you are without you even noticing.

The Moon generally represents an uncomfortable experience for a querent. Trying to unpick facts from feelings, real life from fantasy, or unfounded fears from legitimate causes for concern is arduous and often painful. Sometimes it can't be done at all, which is confusing to experience, and upsetting to watch. But what The Moon does offer is permission to let the subconscious bubble over. It suggests that perhaps you should stop trying to sweep everything under the rug and instead confront it. Listen to it. Sift through it. I was once taught that one of the best ways to quiet a racing mind was to spend ten minutes writing down all my fears and worries, even the ones that I knew were absurd. Just the act of acknowledging those thoughts out loud or on paper can help to quell them.

And sometimes, though not always, and probably not often, The Moon is something that you want to feel. You might want to dance naked and free in the moonlight. You might want to let your subconscious roam for the night. That is alright too. The Moon would never judge you for that.

QUESTIONS TO ASK WHEN YOU SEE THIS CARD: Have you been having strange dreams? Are you feeling confused or fearful and aren't sure why? Is there anything you're trying to avoid thinking about? How can you listen to yourself more carefully and kindly?

THE SUN (XIX)

JOY, OPTIMISM, PLEASURE, GOOD THINGS, POSITIVITY,
CLARITY, UNCERTAINTY, DENIAL

Here we are, well done, you've found it: arguably the best card in the tarot. This card represents a joy so pure, it is usually depicted with a naked baby gleefully riding on the back of a pony, while a big, smiling sun beams down on him. *That could be you!* says the tarot. Isn't that great? Strip yourself bare (metaphorically)! Let the Sun shine down on your (metaphorically) naked body!

Don't overthink this card: The Sun is here to encourage you to be in the moment, to soak it up for all it's worth and perhaps to radiate out some of that warmth to those around you. The journey through the tarot, and through life, isn't always a picnic so it's nice to encounter a scene of utter joy. Maybe you know what this card means to you already – perhaps you're experiencing a summer in your life right now, when things feel easy, happiness is within reach, plans can be made, and problems have solutions. Or perhaps this card describes your attitude towards life: an ability to always find that invincible inner summer, no matter what the weather's like outside. Either way, the card's message is clear: acknowledge and celebrate that moment, or that skill. Cherish whatever – or whoever – helps you to feel energised and vital.

Of course, even the happiest card in the deck has its challenges. If you're content, The Sun is a lovely and welcome presence in a reading. But when life isn't going quite so smoothly, the appearance of this card can feel like a kick in the teeth, a taunting reminder of something that you don't have right now. If you're unhappy, happiness feels like an exclusive club that you're not part of. Grey days can be made even gloomier by the memories of golden times: 'This was the happiest moment of my life'; 'Yesterday I was happier'; 'Today, I am not happy at all.'

While The Moon taps into the subconscious, The Sun is about the things you can see, recognise, name, and hold in your heart. So, what does this card bring into the light for you? Is it a reflection of how you're feeling, or does it catch on something tender? What will you do with those feelings?

Some people seem to hold the inner light of The Sun more easily than others. Children, for example, often have it in abundance. Those of us who are older tend to have to cultivate it. For many, The Sun is a practice. The tarot isn't a gratitude journal – we've established that pretty clearly in the previous seventy-five cards. But it still knows the power of taking some time every day to reflect on what's good in your life, what has worked, what is working. The Sun doesn't just live in moments of overwhelming happiness, victory, and extravagantly joyous occasions. It's also in the simpler things that bring pleasure: the light in the late afternoon, a happy exchange with someone in the park, not missing the bus, something you need being exactly where you thought you left it, a day where everything went well, breathing.

QUESTIONS TO ASK WHEN YOU SEE THIS CARD: How do you feel today? Are you happy? Are you able to live in the moment and enjoy feeling content? What brings you joy? What are the small things that you appreciate? Who in your life brings the sunshine to you?

JUDGEMENT (XX)

CONSEQUENCES, KARMA, METAMORPHOSIS, REBIRTH, RECKONINGS, REWARDS, GUILT, ATONEMENT, ABSOLUTION

Judgement is in many ways the card that people expect Justice to be. On its simplest level, it is the card of getting what you deserve. It is the moment at which you reap what you have sown, when your labour either bears fruit or crumbles into dust. It can be the card of karma and comeuppances: I got mine, and you'll get yours. You cannot run from Judgement, and you cannot hide from it. It's here to deliver the verdict – good or bad. If this card were a meme, it'd be the one that goes: well, well, well, if it isn't the consequences of my own actions.

But this wouldn't be the tarot if there weren't another, more oblique angle to consider. Judgement is about paying your dues, but it's also about what you do after the debt is settled. It's a card of reinvention and rebirth. If you're reading from the Rider Waite Smith, the symbolism is heavy-handed: behold, a group of dead people break out of their coffins and rise up, hands raised to the sky! This is one of the places where the iconography hasn't aged well. Contemporary audiences, upon seeing it, often go to: zombie apocalypse. But, if you're familiar with the Christian tradition you will – correctly! – identify the scene as Judgement Day, which involves a lot less brain-eating and a lot more opportunity to ascend to a higher plane of spiritual fulfilment. Accordingly, many modern decks choose images of secular reincarnation or metamorphosis: friendly ghosts, snakes and butterflies, rather than reanimated corpses.

When Judgement appears in a reading, it's often a chance to look back, and to think about clean slates and the laying to rest of burdens. It has a more complicated relationship with change and transformation than Death, for example, because it's not just about an ending. It's about the weight of experience, know-ledge, and shame that a person can gather up and carry with them. It is the penultimate card of the Major Arcana: it comes at the end of a long journey, and it is an acknowledgment of how difficult that journey might have been. You will have made some mistakes, and it's right that you should own them – but they needn't define you. Judgement feels in some ways like a more substantial, more deeply carved version of the Sixes of the Minor Arcana. It sits at the intersection of past, present, and future, and asks: what will you take and what will you leave behind? Is there some excess baggage that doesn't need to come on the next leg of the journey?

It can be a little bit too easy, I think, to allow this card to speak only of earning adulation or retribution. There's room for being pleased with yourself, of course, and for celebrating who you're becoming over time. Vengeance also has a place here (within reason) and Judgement can certainly invite you to hold yourself to account, to make a reckoning of your actions and behaviours. But its greatest gift is absolution. It's a card that allows you to make peace with yourself, to stop revisiting old hurts and mistakes and regrets. It invites you to shed your old skin and promises that soon you will emerge again, freshly made, and glittering with possibility.

QUESTIONS TO ASK WHEN YOU SEE THIS CARD: What have you done and what do you think you deserve? What burdens are you carrying with you? Is there something stopping you from taking a breath and starting again? Do you feel the need for revenge? Who would you become if nothing was holding you back?

THE WORLD (XXI)

COMPLETION, FULFILMENT, ENLIGHTENMENT, UNITY, SUCCESS,
ENDINGS, BEGINNINGS, CYCLES, TRAJECTORIES, PROGRESS, DECLINE

They say that history repeats itself. It's a notion that appears over and over again in art, culture, philosophy, and scientific theory: the idea that perhaps all of time is a wheel, ever-turning, on which history is endlessly replaying. Off the top of my head, I could probably name three novels, two plays, one film, plus (bonus!) a popular 90s TV show in which this is a central conceit – and in all likelihood, you could too. These are very good references to have when you encounter The World.

This is the final card of the Major Arcana, and it represents the end of a journey. This is the denouement – a chance for you to consider the strands of your story and to figure out how to resolve them. In the simplest interpretations, it brings a moment of completion. This can be a very satisfying moment indeed, one that represents fulfilment, accomplishment, maybe even enlightenment. Like the Tens of Cups and Pentacles, it speaks to unity and self-knowledge, and offers a chance to reflect on what you've achieved and how you got there (nice). But, unlike them, The World is a Major, and that's only the tip of its iceberg. So, are you ready to go deeper?

In the tarot, since this card is the finishing line, it is also the starting block. Like a snake biting its tail, it brings us right back to where we started, fresh-faced and foolish. The World keeps on turning: it is a cycle which in some ways has no beginning and no end, but at the same time very clearly has both. As with life, so it is with tarot: there is always a new story waiting to unfold. The World congratulates you on having completed this orbit and then asks, what next? Are you ready to begin again?

Something that's true in almost all fiction that posits that time is circular – and which I think speaks to the very heart of this card – is that the cycles of time are never a string of identical loops marching off into the future. They have a changing trajectory: each time you go around the carousel, things either get better or worse, depending on your actions. The World tells you that you have that power over your own life. It isn't just the moment of completion; it's also when you get to decide how you'll approach your next run. Will you do better or worse this time around? Some parts of your pattern will feel familiar – but what have you learnt that might help you change them? Are there any ruts which, if you're not careful, you might carve even more deeply?

When people say that history repeats itself, they often do so sadly, or with a sigh of resignation, or a note of foreboding. This is the tarot's way of reminding you that it doesn't have to be like that. You can learn from what's gone before, and from your own experiences, and use what you know to change your path. It can be tempting to decide that things will only ever get worse; that we're sinking, slowing, sliding inexorably towards the end. But, like The Fool (who, in a peculiar way, comes next), The World looks upwards. The World asks: what if you were to rise instead?

QUESTIONS TO ASK WHEN YOU SEE THIS CARD: Have you come to the end of something, or has something finally come to fruition? Do you feel that an important journey is complete? What did you learn and how will you use it? How do you feel about the future?

With The World, you have reached the end not just of the Major Arcana, but also the seventy-eight cards of the tarot deck. It's an appropriate card to encounter last, speaking as it does to cycles: to completion and to beginning again. We said it at the start of the deck, and we say it again at the end: there is always more to learn about each of these cards, and always more stories to be told. But, by now, you should know enough to be able to try reading tarot (if you haven't already). To help you, at the back of this book is a quick guide to the cards at a glance with short prompts to remind you of the core of each card's meaning.

The next step, if you are ready, is to take what you know and apply it to sequences and patterns of cards. There are endless combinations of cards that can emerge in a reading – and no book that could give you an authoritative answer on how each of the cards interacts with all of the others. That's up to you – and arguably it's the best bit of tarot.

CHAPTER 11

Simple Readings

Throughout the card descriptions, we've talked about how the position of a card in a spread might affect the way it's interpreted – whether its light or its shadow side is prominent. Here, we'll take you through some practical advice on beginning to read the cards in sequence, and some spreads that have served us well.

It is perfectly possible to read the tarot just by pulling cards – one, two, a handful – and opening your mind to the possibilities therein: looking for connections and patterns, seeking out relationships between the cards, and asking yourself or your querent if anything particularly stands out for you. We quite often use this method for more discursive, casual readings: it's loose and lovely and allows you to explore all of the cards' different sides and meanings.

However, most of the time – particularly if you're starting out – a more formal spread is your best friend. A tarot spread provides a structure for you to work with or against (*very* The Hierophant): it helps to focus the question you're asking or the issue you're exploring, and it guides the ways in which you might interpret each card. Choosing or creating the right spread for a particular moment can take a little bit of practice, which is also why it's handy to have a few memorised. You can do simple one- or two-card readings in a few minutes, or really bed down with a ten- or twelve-card spread if you have the time.

At its heart, a spread is just the pattern in which you lay cards down: each position in the pattern has a significance which helps you to interpret the card. You, or your querent, can pull cards from the deck one at a time, knowing what position each represents (for example, you might say, 'please pick a card to represent a challenge that you're facing'), or the cards can be picked and laid face down in the correct pattern without talking through the positions beforehand. Once the pattern is complete, you should turn all of the cards over at once and spend a moment taking them in before you begin to read. In this moment, look and see what story they tell together, whether there are any clear patterns and trends. Are there many cards of the same suit? Is any suit wholly absent? What is the mix of Majors or Minors like? Does anything particularly stand out as a big or strange card?

There are some commonly used spreads, which we'll take you through, but this is an aspect of tarot reading where you can be very creative and explore – so we'll also explain the ways in which you can come up with your own patterns. There are plenty of communities online which share new ideas for spreads, and we'd encourage exploring them to see if anything chimes with you. Believe it or not, Pinterest is also a gold mine for inspiration (turns out it's not just recipes and interiors after all), and there are rich seams to mine in seasonal spreads too – a spread for the full moon, or for an equinox, for example. This is one of the tarot's most playful aspects, and we encourage you to embrace it!

TWO-CARD READINGS

Sometimes you don't want a full meal, you want a snack. Two-card readings offer you exactly that: a tasty tarot morsel that allows someone to sample the menu without taking up hours of your day. They're an excellent way to test your knowledge of the deck when you're just getting started, or to dip your toe into understanding how different cards interact with one another. A word of warning, though: two-card spreads are like HIIT classes for occultists: they're quick, but deceptively intense.

You / Your problem: This is technically the centre point of the Celtic Cross (a spread that you'll learn more about in a few pages) and it can be a useful mini reading. One card represents the querent, the other represents the heart of a challenge that they're facing.

Good / Bad: A simple spread for looking at a situation that you face – whether that's taking a job, going to a party, or moving house. This is a great way of exploring what might be good about it, and what might be really bad about it.

Sun / Moon: A spread that we came up with for an event years ago and of which we have become very fond. In this instance, you ask a querent to draw a sun card for something that they should lean into and embrace in their life, and a moon card for something that they might not have noticed but which could be influencing them.

Your hidden strength / Your hidden weakness: Why not get personal with your querent with this high-risk, high-reward spread? It can lead to wonderfully candid conversations about personality and what makes people tick. Handled clumsily, though, it can come across as a character assassination. Exercise caution.

In the blue corner / In the red corner: Got a thorny problem that you can't make sense of, or a difficult decision with no clear answer? Use the tarot kind of like *Street Fighter* – pick two cards to represent different aspects of the issue, or different choices, and let them battle it out. We wish you a quick and conclusive K.O.

Tarot remix: Not technically a spread, but a very good use of two cards is basically to see them as a partnership – a sort of occult CELEBRITY x SHOE BRAND, or tarot cronut (for the uninitiated: that's a croissant–doughnut hybrid, and it has a very interesting texture). What do the two cards have in common? Where is there tension? What's their lovechild? What do these two energies create together?

THREE-CARD READINGS

The three-card spread is arguably the bread and butter of tarot readings. It's simple to use and easy for a querent to follow. There are enough cards for there to be interesting dynamics between them, without it all becoming too complicated. It can stretch into a long conversation, or be compressed into a short one. And three is just quite a satisfying number.

Past / Present / Future: The training-wheels spread for all first-time readers! I think you can probably work out how to use this one.

Origin / Situation / Direction: Similar to the above, but slightly less rooted in fortune-telling if you don't want to read futures – it's more about someone's trajectory in life. Where have they come from? Where are they now? Where are they going to go if they continue unchecked?

You / Me / Us: A classic for reading for a pair of friends, lovers, or otherwise – it can be the reader and the querent, or a reading for two people. Each person pulls one card to reflect their own attitude, and then together they pull a third for their shared dynamic. Grab the popcorn – this one often starts fascinating conversations.

Where you are / What you've learnt / What you still need to: A reading that can be applied to any number of situations: romance, work, personal development. This can be a good spread to help you think about how the cards' meanings flex when approached through new angles.

Stop doing / Start doing / Continue doing: Yes, you might recognise this from professional appraisals. But it works really well for tarot reading, too. (And yes, of course we've both occasionally considered using it as the basis of an annual review to see what happens.)

What you feel / What you think / What you hope: A sort of heart, mind, soul spread that can create opportunities to discuss conflicting desires and unknot problems. Apply it to anything: a relationship, a job you've been offered, the purchase of a new pair of shoes, a new idea that you're thinking of pursuing.

THE CELTIC CROSS

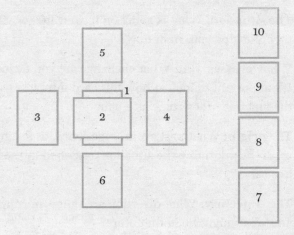

For anyone who wants an in-depth tarot reading, the Celtic Cross is your first and most faithful friend. This big lad of a spread is beloved among tarot readers because it is so detailed and comprehensive. Expect a reading with this many cards to take half an hour at the very least.

With the Celtic Cross, you read the cards in a specific order – and it can be helpful to go through them one by one with your querent to start the reading. But the real art to this spread is how much scope it gives you to explore the interactions between different cards: the patterns and the ways in which they relate to one another.

The spread itself has two component parts, the Cross (six cards) and the Pillar (four cards). The first section is introspective, exploring what's going on for a querent and why, while the second is more active and focuses on new possibilities. Both also work as smaller spreads in their own right, and you can even subdivide them down into smaller sections.

The Cross:

1. **The situation:** What is going on in your life, or what is preoccupying you, right now?

2. **What 'crosses' you:** What challenge are you facing? It's important to look at how this card interacts with the first one – they come as a pair.

3. **The origin:** What past event, experience, or feeling might be informing the situation described in the first two cards?

4. **The trajectory:** What direction are things moving in, and what might lie in the future?

5. **Conscious:** What are you aware of in this situation, what is driving your behaviour or your beliefs about it?

6. **Subconscious:** What might you not yet be aware of that influences your thinking? How does this contrast or compliment card number 5, the conscious influence?

The Pillar:

7. **What you are bringing to the situation:** How does your attitude affect the situation, or how might it? Sometimes, this position is understood as a word of advice.

8. **External influences:** What's going on around you? How do other people influence the situation? What's their point of view?

9. **Hopes and/or fears:** What do you wish for? How closely is it intertwined with what you fear? How does this card relate to card number 6, the subconscious influences at play? Does it clarify the hopes and/or fears card at all?

10. **Advice:** Traditionally, this is an 'outcome' card which is supposed to indicate what the consequences of your situation could be. But, as we've established, the tarot does not get to decide how your life is going to turn out! We tend to read this position as 'something to consider'. It's worth looking at card number 5, what you're aware of about this situation, when you read this card to see whether the ideas are aligned or in conflict.

CREATING YOUR OWN SPREADS

Once you've got the hang of using spreads to guide your readings, it's time to experiment with creating your own. Sometimes, this can be as simple as adapting something you've already used, or combining the juiciest aspects of different spreads. And sometimes it can be a chance for your imagination to run wild. There really isn't anything you're not allowed to do in spreads – I once saw a spread online called What The Fuck?, in which you were instructed to pull four cards: one for each word and one for the question mark. All that really matters is whether or not it works for you.

The key to a good spread is to ensure that each position has a very clearly defined role in the pattern. Usually, it's worth having at least one card that represents the present moment or situation, something that roots you to the here and now. While some tarot readers may disagree with us here, we find that yes / no questions do not work at all (the tarot abhors specificity!), so you're looking for statements that have the right balance of being focused and open-ended. Given that the tarot is so rooted in archetypes and experiences, spreads tend to work best if each of the positions represents either an aspect of the self, an attitude, or a suggestion.

On a practical level, if you're trying to come up with a new spread, the easiest thing to do is test it out on yourself and see what happens. Do the positions and angles you've thought of seem too broad or too narrow when you pull cards against them? Do you feel like they offer richness and provoke conversation, or are they a bit oblique and hard to understand? If it's not working, that's fine! It's your spread! You can alter it until it does!

One tip we feel we must offer about creating a spread: write it down somewhere you can find it – even if you're going to try it right away. Fiona and I have been using the same spread for onstage interviews for years. After a summer of doing the same spread over and over again, we're both convinced that we could never, ever forget it. And yet, every winter, it somehow vanishes from memory. And so, like clockwork, come the spring there is a frantic rummaging through of paperwork while we both try to find the one ancient archive card on which the original spread was stored ahead of our first performance. (If either of us were more like the Knight of Pentacles, we'd have a better filing system, but alas it is not so.)

And finally, whether it's your own spread or a well-known one, we always say: if in doubt, introduce an (additional) element of chaos. It never hurts to pull a wild card – a card to represent the unexpected, something you've not yet seen, but which might have power – right at the very end. What, as we often ask ourselves, could possibly go wrong?

CHAPTER 12

Practical Magic

N ow that you've met all of the cards of the deck and been introduced to some common spreads, the only thing left to do is: give it a go. The tarot is something that takes practice, and at which you can only get better over time. In other words, it's time to channel your inner Eight of Pentacles.

To help you get the most out of it, here are our tried-and-tested techniques for committing the cards to memory and getting to know them on your own terms, a few tips on giving your first readings for other people – and as some advice on how to choose and care for your tarot deck.

Reading cuts of the deck

There's no avoiding the fact that a tarot deck contains a lot of cards. It takes time to get to know them all, and trying to memorise seventy-eight sets of meanings is quite the task.

But, as the old saying goes, the best way to eat an elephant is one bite at a time. With the tarot it's the same: for those who don't feel that they can take the plunge with the full deck – which is pretty much everyone – there is an option to ease oneself in more slowly. The tarot is like a lovely occult satsuma: it is already split into convenient segments! You wouldn't try to put a whole satsuma in your mouth, would you? (Please say no.) Well, you can approach the cards in the same way. As you know, the Minors are governed by some clear patterns and rules, and the twenty-two Majors form a linear narrative – so, all you need to do is to split the deck into its five key chapters along those lines. Then you familiarise yourself with and read from one of these cuts at a time until you feel confident with their meanings. This is not sacrilege – it is practical and it works.

The other great advantage of learning with cuts from the deck is that you are, statistically, far more likely to see all of the cards. When you're working with a full deck, there might be weeks or months between glimpses of a certain card. But when you're working with fifteen or twenty-two, it's much harder for any of the little scamps to hide. This technique flushes them out, and it gives you more of a chance to get to know everyone.

Keeping a tarot journal

Part of learning the tarot is learning the meanings that are ascribed to each of the cards. And part of it – in some ways, the more interesting part – is developing your own under-standing of each card's symbolism. Your personal responses to the stories that each one tells is what will add richness to your readings, and deepen your relationship with the practice over time. Decks such as the Rider Waite Smith are designed in such a way that all the basic symbols you need to be able to understand them are literally *on* them – and, as the good tarot scholars that we are, we would encourage you to commit those commonly agreed meanings to memory. But we're also keen to stress that, over time, a significant portion of your knowledge of the cards, and your enjoyment of them, will come from being able to read and interpret them through the lens of your own experiences and ideas.

One of the best things that you can do, both to cement the standard meanings of the cards in your mind, and to help you gather your own interpretations, is to get into the habit of keeping a tarot journal. It doesn't have to be anything fancy: just a notebook in which you can keep a record of your thoughts and impressions of readings you give and receive; the conversations and questions that arose from them; and what light the readings shed on the relationships between cards, as well as their individual meanings. Writing a diary is a helpful way of processing your thoughts and feelings and a tarot journal is no different. It can be hard to remember the finer detail of a reading once you've come away from it – sometimes you might leave with the impression that you've had a reading filled with Swords when, in reality, there were only two Swords cards and you just fixated on them. You don't need to go into endless detail in an entry – treat each reading like a day, simply flagging the cards that were noteworthy, surprising or vexing, and adding some context, is enough.

If you're getting started, a journal exercise that we both found very valuable is giving yourself single-card readings on a regular schedule. You set aside a moment – whether that's every morning, or just once or twice a week, depending on when you can make time. On each occasion, draw one card to represent the day – think of it like a little emotional weather forecast, a meditation, or a North Star by which to navigate. Focus on the image for a few minutes. Without looking it up, note down what it surfaces for you, even if you can't remember anything about what it's supposed to mean. First thought, best thought, as Allen Ginsberg would say. What do you think this one could be about? What questions does it bring up? Is there anything in particular that it calls to mind? Once you've recorded your first impressions of the card, read or reread its description in a reference book (hi) or online and add any further notes. You need only spend a few minutes on each reading and in no time at all – well, maybe a few months – you'll have worked your way through the whole deck, and it'll be feeling far more familiar to you than when you started out.

Practising on people

Denis Wood, author of *The Power of Maps*, once made the point that street signs are for strangers: when a place is a part of you, you don't need them to help you locate yourself. The same is true of the tarot. For a while, having a guide is the best way to give each card a meaning and get a feel for the territory. But there will come a time when you've got most of the landmarks and major causeways committed to memory, and you're ready to start wandering, and creating your own, unique internal map of wherever this place is.

When I say 'wandering', what I mean is 'reading' – specifically, for other people, rather than just pulling cards for yourself. Jen and I have long worked as a pair not just because it's fun but because it has helped us both to become better tarot readers. Nothing makes you put the guide book down and engage with what is in front of you quite like having another human being with their own stories and questions. And the more you practice, the more fluent you'll become. So, read for friends, read for your partner, read for family, read for colleagues, read for your pets, read for more seasoned tarot readers. Join a local tarot circle, ask for volunteers in tarot forums. Make sure, of course, that they're willing. And make sure to tell them that you will not be portending deaths, nor will you be exposing all of their deepest secrets and insecurities because you literally cannot. People tend to find this reassuring.

Of course, your early card readings won't be perfect. Sometimes you'll find yourself stumped. Sometimes you'll mis-remember cards. And sometimes you'll be so overwhelmed by the spread in front of you that you'll say something that barely makes sense. It happens! But over time, you'll become more confident, and realise it's not about trying to recite a meaning from a book with 100 per cent, word-perfect accuracy. It's about using the cards to build a story. It's about listening and interacting and having a meaningful conversation. It's about sharing your stories and experiences. And it's easier to do than you imagine. But, just in case, here are five pieces of advice for your first readings:

Tell them you're new to this. One day you may be A Great Mystic but, for now, let people know that you're practising. Perhaps you can work through the bits that don't make sense together. And perhaps you can laugh about it if it all goes wrong.

Let them peer behind the veil. If you're reading for someone who isn't into the tarot, talk them through what you're going to do, the deck you're using, and what they can expect. In fact, in our experience, people enjoy tarot readings far more when they have some idea of what's going on.

Ask questions. The best thing about freely admitting that you are not a psychic tarot reader is that you do not have to act as though you are one. You do not have all the answers, but you DO have all the questions. Ask them! (Just don't force a response.)

Say if you're stuck. It happens to the best of us. Three Knights will eventually show up in a reading, or you'll get The Devil crossed with The Sun and you'll find yourself grasping for what this might mean in the context of someone's impending nuptials. Don't panic. Explore what you do know, and admit to what you don't. And if it looks like the other person is hating the whole experience... you can just stop.

Let them take a picture. For one thing, tarot cards are pretty. For another, sometimes people like to muse on what you've told them in their own time, or google the cards, or look them up in a book to learn more. This is an easy way to help.

Patterns, trends, neighbours

We've repeatedly referenced the patterns of the tarot in terms of how they can help you to understand (and memorise) the cards' meanings, but that's not the only reason to pay attention to them. They can also be significant when it comes to interpreting how cards interact with one another. There are a few common themes that are noticeable, or worth considering when you are giving readings:

Suit-mates: The easiest pattern to see is when a lot of cards from the same suit appear in a reading – or if there are a cluster of Majors. And the conclusion to be drawn is also quite straightforward: the energy of that suit is uppermost for the querent, or the situation they're facing. The suit might seem surprising at first – for example, a run of Cups in a reading about someone's work – but it's worth trying to unpick the significance (in that instance, it might lead you to discuss whether or not a person's job is influencing their emotional state). And if it's a lot of Majors, it tends to mean that Significant Occurrences are afoot.

Neighbours: Since all of the cards in both the Minors and the Majors can be read as a journey, with each card building on its predecessor, finding cards that are consecutive in the deck can lead you to consider what the querent's trajectory overall is. Are they making progress forwards, or are they falling back? Don't forget that in the Swords and the Wands, there are some places (the Nines and Tens) where backwards is good. It can also be valuable to bear the cards' neighbours in mind even when you don't see them: if The Star appears, for example, it can be useful to speak to a querent about its relationship with The Tower and The Moon. How does this healing, constructive moment relate to having experienced unexpected changes or difficult shifts in their world view? Are there things that still feel unresolved or confusing, which are still preying on their subconscious?

Matching jerseys: Like players in a very bizarre sporting league, the majority of the cards of the tarot are emblazoned with numbers. So what happens when more than one with the same number turns up? This one can be a bit of a red herring, unless you're an expert numerologist. The numerical positions of the Minor Arcana are significant, and cards with the same position share a common theme. But, because of the very different natures of the suits and the irregular numbers of the Majors (i.e. the fact that it contains a zero), parallels aren't always illuminating, especially if you're looking at them through the lens of a spread. There are times when you might want to pay attention, though: a Ten of Wands and a Ten of Swords appearing as a double act, for example, might open up conversations about feeling overwhelmed and unhappy. Three Aces in a spread could point to an abundance of potential, but also a lack of direction. I'd advise you to look for any unusual groupings, but to focus more on neighbours than matches when it comes to card numbers.

Court factions: It's generally not a treat when you get a party of court cards in a spread. So many competing personalities! So much potential for conflict and drama! Is this something that feels familiar to a querent right now? Do they feel like they're being pulled in lots of different directions by lots of different people? Or do they feel like they're at war with themself? Try to see where the court cards might support one another, or where they might be at odds, particularly within the context of the other cards. Two or three Knights in a reading? That might suggest a need to slow down and take a breath. The King of one suit and the Queen of another: do those cards balance one another out, or are they bringing out the worst in each other?

Major and Minor siblings: These ones are the hardest to spot at first, but do tend to become clearer over time as you get to know the cards better. All of the Majors have corresponding siblings in the Minors: cards that have a similar meaning, but expressed at a rather quieter volume. For the astrologists out there, the formal pairings are based on which zodiac sign each card is governed by. The Devil, for example, has a sister in the Queen of Pentacles, because they are both Capricorns. (Fiona and I are also both Capricorns – read into that what you will.) When these dyads appear, the best thing to do is to really pay attention to the common theme. There are also places where you'll see echoes and similarities between cards because of the positions in which they appear in a spread, even if they aren't siblings – for example, when two Minor Arcana cards seem to be aligning. Allow yourself to explore those connections: let the cards enter into dialogue with one another and give new dimensions to one another's meanings, rather than being compartmentalised. This can add real richness and nuance to your interpretations.

Choosing your tarot deck

There are hundreds, if not thousands, of tarot decks available now – many of them created by independent artists and designers who have reinterpreted the tarot in different ways. And one of the great joys of the tarot is discovering a new deck, reading through it and seeing how each card has been depicted. Once you're steady on your cartomancy feet, we'd highly recommend looking at different tarot designs and finding something that speaks to you.

Maybe it'll speak to you because you think its interpretation of tarot symbols is on point, or maybe it'll be because you think it's really pretty. Maybe it's something else entirely! Whatever the reason, follow your instincts. You might end up with lots of different decks that you use on different occasions, or just one or two that you return to over and over again. A word of warning to the would-be tarot purchaser: do be careful to check if you're buying a pip deck. Pips are tarot decks in which only the Major Arcana cards are fully illustrated, while the other fifty-six cards are indicated only by their number and their suit. These are great in some circumstances (no pictures of dead people with ten swords in their backs) but obviously somewhat more difficult for beginners who are still learning the meanings of all the cards

You might also have heard of the tradition, or superstition, that you shouldn't buy a tarot deck for yourself. We wholeheartedly support this tradition – because what's nicer than a gift from a friend of a lovely new tarot deck? But it's totally fine to buy your own cards. The cards will never know. It should also be noted that what someone else chooses for you might not be what you would have chosen for yourself. An example: my grandfather once presented me with a Kama Sutra tarot deck that he found at a car boot sale. (The person who sold it to him insisted that it had never been used, but I remain suspicious.)

Shuffling the deck

You can shuffle and cut the deck however you like – and if you're very bad at shuffling cards and maybe sometimes drop them, that's still fine. Some readers prefer to deal the cards for their querents, others fan the cards out then smush them around (I believe this is the technical term, though croupiers would call this washing the cards), and ask the querents to select their own. The only consistent, if fairly obvious, point is that the cards tend to be presented for selection face down so that the person being read for can't see which one is which and spoil the big reveal.

Caring for your cards

Storing cards is another topic around which there are a number of traditions. Some prefer to treat their tarot decks very carefully, wrapping them in silk, not allowing other people to touch them. Others treat their deck in much the same way they would a pack of playing cards – it's somewhere in the bottom of their bag, along with dried-up ballpoint pens, a cigarette lighter, tampons, and six years' worth of receipts. There is no right answer. If you feel that your cards are objects that should be clean and crisp, then follow that instinct. If you feel more comfortable with a battered, lived-in deck with soft fuzzy edges and miscellaneous ink stains, it's an equally valid approach. Maybe you'll end up with a collection of decks, some of which get the special treatment, and others of which are daily workhorses. When it comes to tarot storage, there are really no rules except for the rules you make for yourself.

And the only rule we have made for ourselves is this: if we are taking tarot cards somewhere with a risk of inclement weather, such as a music festival during a British summer, we first place each deck in a glamorous, resealable sandwich bag. The tarot may be ancient, but we have learnt the hard way that it is not at all waterproof.

CHAPTER 13

Where Next?

We hope that we've introduced you to the tarot in a way that has helped you to see how fascinating, illuminating and, indeed, magical it can be – and that you're ready to try it for yourself. But we're only one small part of a wide, diverse, and ever-changing community of people who have found something to love about the tarot, and we encourage you to explore this world further.

TAROT DECKS

We couldn't possibly do justice to all of the different decks out there, but here are some that we've enjoyed reading from and exploring over the years.

Decks which stay close to the Rider Waite Smith iconography but use their own illustration style:

The Aquarian Tarot: A beautiful and simple art nouveau style deck.

Modern Witch Tarot, by Lisa Sterle: A deck populated by diverse female characters.

Dali Tarot: It's the tarot, but as Salvador Dali imagined it! Surprisingly un-surreal.

The Magician Longs To See Tarot, by Benjamin Mackey: In this one, the cult series *Twin Peaks* is mapped onto a tarot deck – and it works impressively well. The Log Lady is, naturally, The High Priestess. It is famously impossible to get hold of (Fiona still periodically checks eBay to see if she might find one second hand), but Mackey has the full deck displayed on his website, for your delectation.

Decks which include different visual interpretations (and sometimes card names):

Spolia Tarot, by Jen May and Jessa Crispin: One of our all-time favourites, this deck looks as though it has been collaged out of the most sumptuous materials imaginable.

The Wild Unknown Tarot, by Kim Krans: This pen-and-ink style deck draws its characters from the natural world, replacing the human characters with more abstract images of animals and plants.

Cosmic Woman Tarot, by Lisa Junius: An easy-to-read deck populated only by nude female characters in a starlit sky. Simple clean lines and a calming blue colour palette.

Circo Tarot, by Marisa de la Peña: A playful tarot with a circus theme, this deck is brightly coloured and joyful – but don't be fooled, it still has an appropriately feral edge.

Akamara Tarot: A gold-gilt 78-card deck that pays homage to the gift of divinity and variety in the spiritualities that make up the African Diaspora.

Carnival at the End of the World, and The Drowning World Tarot, by Kahn & Selesnick: These two decks are creative in their visual interpretations – creepy, yet stunning.

Tarot del Fuego, by Ricardo Cavolo: As with all of Cavolo's illustrations, this deck is bright and bold and every single card has a lot (a LOT) more eyes than you might expect.

Tarot of the Old Path, by Sylvia Gainsford: An early 90s deck designed for Pagan readers with a glorious medieval fair aesthetic. One card is supposedly a portrait of Barbara Streisand.

The Numinous Tarot, by Cedar McCloud: This beautiful deck reimagines the tarot in a way that is more inclusive of gender, race and identity. The Empress, for example, becomes The Nurturer, shifting the focus from the mother figure to the idea that we should tend and care for ourselves and others, perhaps as we might tend to a garden.

Omni Tarot, by Olivia M. Healy: A modern deck that still feels timeless, with long-legged, usually solo and usually female characters leaping through the cards.

Thoth Tarot, by Aleister Crowley and Lady Frieda Harris: A slightly different deck structure to the RWS, and one which is used as an alternative blueprint by a number of modern designs. The illustration style is mid-century occult: folkloric rather than dark and twisty. It should be noted, though, that Crowley himself is a controversial and even problematic figure, and we wouldn't recommend delving into his wider work as an occultist without learning a little more about him first.

Pip decks and short decks:

Pip decks in the tarot are those in which only the Majors are fully illustrated. They can be very rewarding to read from once you know the cards well – and there are some beautiful examples out there. But do be aware that, with these, there's no visual prompt to remind you of the meanings in the Minors: only the card's suit and its position.

There are also some decks which only contain the Majors, or which compress the seventy-eight cards down somewhat. We mostly avoid reading with these, but there are occasions when it feels right – and they're often the most wonderful works of art.

Tarot de Marseille: One of the oldest tarot decks known, and with a slightly different structure to the RWS (which influenced Crowley's Thoth) – we rarely read from it, but it's interesting to look at.

The Nomad Tarot, by Jennifer Dranttel: This Pacific northwestern-inspired pip deck takes a bit of practice, but is a calm and beautiful reading experience once you know it.

Le Tarot de L'étoile Cachée: This delicate deck of only the Majors is matte black card, detailed in clean silver linework. It's almost too precious to use (but you totally can).

The Autonomic Tarot, by Sophy Hollington and David Keenan: A wild and playful deck, which is compressed into thirty cards. Well worth exploring once you're feeling confident.

Black Power Tarot, by King Khan: Musician King Khan, a tarot student of the filmmaker Alejandro Jodorowski, chose twenty-six African Americans to figure in his Tarot deMarseilles-inspired deck. He has spoken in interviews about choosing people whom he felt followed a true path of illumination despite being born in a country that was against them.

NB. While some tarot decks are always around, those which are created by independent designers tend to have much smaller print runs, and aren't always available to buy. For such decks, look for second-hand sales. It's also worth following their creators online for announcements about new releases.

RESOURCES AND GUIDES

Each tarot reader brings their own experiences and interpretations to the cards, and our book is no different. If you would like to continue your tarot journey, here are some of the books, courses (online and in person), websites, and people that we'd recommend exploring, for more perspectives and depth.

Books:

***Seventy-Eight Degrees of Wisdom: A Book of Tarot* by Rachel Pollack (1980):** This book has been described as the bible of tarot readers. Pollack is considered one of the world's foremost experts on the tarot. Her erudite and detailed guide explores the cards' origins, meanings, symbolism, and applications.

***The Creative Tarot: A Modern Guide to an Inspired Life* by Jessa Crispin (2016):** A sharp, entertaining, and culturally rich guide to unlocking your creativity through tarot readings. Crispin is an author, critic, and she was the editor-in-chief of the webzine *Bookslut*.

***Queering the Tarot* by Cassandra Snow (2019):** The tarot is a tool for self-discovery, healing, growth, and empowerment. Yet a casual glance at the Rider Waite Smith deck shows you a world that seems overwhelmingly white, European, and heterosexual. Snow deconstructs the meanings of the cards in ways that make space for conversations about sexuality, gender, and gender-queering, sources of oppression and empowerment, and much more.

***Tarot For Change: Using the Cards For Self-Care, Accept-
ance and Growth*** **by Jessica Dore (2021):** Dore's thoughtful
meditations on tarot cards have resonated with thousands of
readers on Twitter. In this book, Dore breathes life into the
language of the cards by drawing on her experience as a social
worker and her many years in psychological publishing.

Ignota Books: This glorious small press, run by London-based
Sarah Shin and Ben Vickers, uses magic and myth-making as
prisms to reconsider the world. Among their titles is *Spells:
21st-Century Occult Poetry*, a collection of thirty-six poems
that explore themes of justice in relation to the transformative
power of the occult, and a work of science fiction by the
twelfth-century mystic Hildegard von Bingen and twenty-first-
century writer Huw Lemmey. Wild.

The Castle of Crossed Destinies **by Italo Calvino:** This 1973
novel begins with a meeting among travellers who find that they
are unable to speak after journeying through a forest. Instead,
the characters explain what has happened to them through
tarot cards – with their stories reconstructed by the narrator. It
is a gloriously creative way of using the tarot that also explores
how meaning is created – something to ponder as you learn
more about the tarot and how its usage has evolved over the
centuries.

Courses:

Treadwell's Books, Store Street, London WC1: An occult
bookshop nestled in the heart of Bloomsbury, which also
hosts lectures, classes, and workshops on esoteric matters
including the tarot. It is also the alma mater of your authors.
treadwells-london.com

The Alternative Tarot Course: An online, eight-week, self-study course run by Beth Maiden of Little Red Tarot, that seeks to deepen your tarot practice. Alongside grounding you in the meanings of the cards, Maiden imparts wisdom on how to use tarot for self-care, forming personal rituals, and understanding and reinterpreting the cards, if you have found them 'too straight, too white, too hierarchical, too whatever'. littleredtarot.com

Shops:

Treadwell's Books, Store Street, London WC1: In 2003, the mediaevalist Christina Oakley-Harrington opened Treadwell's, a glorious, thriving esoteric bookshop and cultural centre that sells specialist texts, rare herbs, ceremonial oils, candles, tarot decks, and anything else a modern occultist could possibly desire. The shop also hosts lectures and workshops on subjects from chaos magic to literary witches of the 1920s, herbs, shamanism, and more.

She's Lost Control, Broadway Market, London E8: Jill Urwin left her career in fashion to follow her heart into creating SLC, a conscious lifestyle brand. Here in the peaceful haven of her shop in East London, you can buy candles, ethically sourced crystals, tarot decks, and other tools for spiritual practices. She also throws excellent parties (aura photography anyone?).

HausWitch (online and in Salem, Massachusetts): Lotions, potions – and beechwood cauldron scrubbers too (we guess dishwashers haven't been built with them in mind). An aspirational, inclusive one-stop shop for all of your witch wares. All of the products come from independent makers from around New England and the US. hauswitchstore.com

Little Red Tarot: Now that you are familiar with the cards, it's time for you to find a tarot deck that truly speaks to your soul. And there are few better places to do this than on Little Red Tarot, a UK-based online shop that centres and celebrates queer, trans & BIPOC art and magic. Here you'll find dozens of gorgeous decks for sale and reviewed (always thoughtfully and helpfully) by Beth Maiden, who runs the store. littleredtarot.com

Two Sides Tarot: Another wonderful online portal for tarot deck discovery. Here you'll find a selection of independent and feminist tarot decks, lovingly curated by Marianne in Sydney, Australia. twosidestarot.com

People:

Laetitia Barbier: Barbier is a French tarot reader, art historian, and Head Librarian at Morbid Anatomy in New York. She has discovered and shared hundreds of spectacular and curious images of tarot and obscure fortune-telling decks through her Instagram account. She is now turning these cards into a visual history of the tarot.

Rachel Howe: Also known as Small Spells, Howe is a Los Angeles-based artist, tarot reader, astrologer, and tattoo artist. She believes readings should be empowering experiences that help querents find their way to healing.

Chinggay Labrador: A Manila-based artist and reader who runs Practical Magic, an accessible web resource for all things tarot.

Sullivan Hismans: Tarot Sheet Revival is Hismans's labour of love: explore his handcrafted, recreated versions of the earliest printed tarot decks.

QUESTIONS TO ASK YOURSELF

Learning to read the tarot is a journey with no end – it is something that you can dip into and out of whenever you wish, and it's a practice that grows with you. Over time, your understanding of different cards will click into focus, or you'll find new meanings buried in their depths. And you should never feel afraid to try something new with them: tarot reading is an evolving practice and has always had something of play in it, something of curiosity and creativity and inventiveness. Collect tarot cards, frame them, meditate on them, swap them, post them to friends, use them as writing prompts, or play games with them – the choice is yours.

We'll leave you with a few questions to help you explore how you want to use the tarot, and what direction your practice might take from here.

What have you enjoyed about exploring the cards? What has felt uncomfortable?

Do you like the idea of reading for other people, or as a personal and private practice?

How does understanding the tarot affect how you experience a reading?

How do you feel about the idea of fortune-telling? Does it scare you? Are you curious?

Are there any ways you can imagine using the cards differently? Will you try it?

How relatable have you found the cards – both their visual depictions and the interpretations? How might you reinterpret them?

How often do you read for yourself? How do you feel after a tarot reading?

What do you hope to get from reading the tarot? Does it feel possible now?

The Cards At A Glance

The **Minor Arcana**	ACE source of the suit, an abundance of it	TWO daily tasks of the suit, building or blocking	THREE an experience that embodies the suit
WANDS fire energy spirit doing	Power is in your hands – but where will you direct it?	A decision that must be made in order to progress.	To achieve your goals, you need a plan. Do you?
CUPS water heart feeling creating	Powerful creative or emotional potential, an awakening.	Positive unions: love, a marriage, a creative project.	Community and friendship and the support it brings.
SWORDS air intellect mind thinking	A Eureka! moment of clarity and the chance to act on it.	Conviction and confidence to break a stalemate.	Pain, heartache, and its role in building you.
PENTACLES earth body being manifesting	Fertile ground in which to plant a seed and hope.	Are you balancing things . . . or are you just juggling?	Collaboration, working with others to build something.

FOUR	FIVE	SIX	SEVEN
a moment to reflect along the way	discomfort, conflict, or difficulties	a shift in the balance of power	evaluation and decisions
Celebrations are in order. Throw a glorious party.	Conflicting opinions and tension that can be beneficial.	Look how far you've come! Where next? Onwards!	Choosing your battles and living by your principles.
New things are being offered. But do you want them?	Loss. Mourn it, but don't forget what you still have.	Nostalgia and revisiting good times goneby.	Fantasy! Explore your wildest dreams! Rrrr!
Silence and mindfulness. You've earnt a rest.	Dehumanising others, lacking empathy and care.	Taking what you've learnt and forging something new	Sometimes you need to be a bit selfish . . . or sneaky.
Stable table, a solid place. But . . . are you bored of it?	Feeling shut out, the only person who isn't included.	Fairness and generosity: your own, or others.'	What's working for you? What isn't? Time to refocus.

The **Minor Arcana** (continued)	**EIGHT** transformative power of the suit	**NINE** steeped in the energy of the suit	**TEN** the ultimate outcome and completion
WANDS fire energy spirit doing	Do it. Do it now. Do it fast. Strike while the anvil is hot.	Doing too much, needing to put something down.	Burnt out and exhausted. Rest is the only solution.
CUPS water heart feeling creating	When you know in your heart that it's time to move on.	Feeling the joy, feeling good, appreciating life.	Love and happiness or creative fulfilment.
SWORDS air intellect mind thinking	Trapped by your thoughts. Only you can free yourself.	Being awoken in the middle of the night by your fears.	It's all gone wrong. The darkness before the dawn.
PENTACLES earth body being manifesting	Be diligent and work hard. Practice makes perfect.	Being Cher: a rich man, independent and successful.	An achievement: wealth, security, material success.

PAGE	KNIGHT	QUEEN	KING
opportunities that aren't bound by rules	the most extra expression of the suit	deep understanding of the suit's energy	mastery of the suit, extending to others
Adventure, wonder and voyages of discovery.	An agent of chaos, for good and for bad. Also – horny.	Charismatic, strong-minded, drawing people in.	Magnetic, dominant and often quite intimidating.
'I just have a lot of feelings'. Hi, it's your subconscious.	Very intense, lots of feelings, wow. A true romantic.	A pure heart! Intuitive, caring, calm and fair.	Emotional self-awareness and benevolence.
A precocious child, full of questions and new ideas.	Quick witted, argumentative, and occasionally cruel.	Independent, clever, perceptive, and self-contained.	True wisdom, earnt rather than claimed, always learning.
Enthusiasm, the doer who needs some guidance.	Earnest and dull and practical: things done properly.	Material comfort, because you're allowed nice things.	Abundance, power, success – also kind of a hoarder.

The
Major Arcana

0. THE FOOL

The beginning of a journey and a call to trust in your instincts. The leap of faith that embraces the unknown and isn't foolish at all.

1. THE MAGICIAN

Agency and belief and confidence. The power to make anything happen. What will you conjure up? Who do you want to be?

2. THE HIGH PRIESTESS

The guardian of the subconscious mind, peeking beyond the veil of the material world. Intuition reigns. What does yours tell you?

3. THE EMPRESS

Fertility and fecundity but not necessarily in the literal sense. Knowing that everything has its season, and grows when it's ready.

4. THE EMPEROR

Authority, power, leadership, the establishment. Yes, it's the patriarchy, but it's also a father figure and a place of safety.

5. THE HIEROPHANT

The structures and traditions that shape us or against which we push: ethics and boundaries; knowledge and hierarchies.

6. THE LOVERS

The establishment of a profound union, or personal values. Is it passionate or harmonious? Is there a choice or a conflict?

7. THE CHARIOT

Riding to victory with a clear sense of purpose and direction. Forging your own path – even if it means swimming against the tide.

8. STRENGTH

It's strength, obviously, but the quiet type that comes from within, from taming your own beasts: determination, courage, patience.

9. THE HERMIT

Time to yourself, to reflect and recharge. Remember, hermits aren't outcasts: others understand and support their need for solitude.

10. WHEEL OF FORTUNE

Things change. Sometimes it's in your favour and sometimes it's not. You can't direct the wind, but you can adjust the sails.

11. JUSTICE

Justice is concerned not with what is fair but with what is right. Strip away feelings and accept the laws of nature and the universe.

12. THE HANGED MAN

Hanged by the foot, not the neck: this is about new perspectives. The cost of knowledge is sacrifice, what will you gain by letting go?

13. DEATH

Endings are necessary, if not always easy – but in death there is always the promise of new life. Is it time to say goodbye?

14. TEMPERANCE

Balance and moderation, often between strongly opposing forces, to create something better. A new insight, or perhaps even art.

15. THE DEVIL

The most powerful beliefs and behaviours are self-reinforcing, repeating patterns. Are you in control, or do they control you?

16. THE TOWER

Total and unexpected destruction – the moment where things fall apart, or are uprooted. Sometimes, it's exactly what's needed.

17. THE STAR

After the fall comes the healing. A card of balance, hope, serenity and self-knowledge – but the sort that tends to be hard-won.

18. THE MOON

Is it real life? Is it all a fantasy? Only the moon knows. A glimpse into your deepest self, where illusions and dreams can run wild.

19. THE SUN

Radiance and joy, a being of pure light. Frolicking in meadows and delighting in everything the world has to offer. Very nice.

20. JUDGEMENT

How have you behaved and how will your actions be judged? A chance to evaluate yourself – and an opportunity for transformation.

21. THE WORLD

The completion of a journey, the end of an act, fulfilment and enlightenment. And, in ending, also a beginning. Here we go again!

References

Published books

Works of fiction

Baum, L. Frank, *The Wizard of Oz* (George M. Hill, 1900)

Carter, Angela, *Angela Carter's Book of Fairy Tales* (Virago, 2005)

Dickens, Charles, *Great Expectations* (1861)

Garner, Alan, *The Owl Service* (William Collins, 1967)

Grahame, Kenneth, *The Wind in the Willows* (Methuen, 1931)

Golding, William, *Lord of the Flies* (Faber & Faber, 1954)

Groff, Lauren, *Matrix* (Penguin Random House, 2021)

Hobb, Robin, *Realm of the Elderlings* Series (Harper Collins, 1995)

Lewis, C.S., *The Lion the Witch and the Wardrobe* (Geoffrey Bles, 1950)

Machado, Carmen Miranda, *In The Dream House* (Graywolf Press, 2019)

Moss, Sarah, *The Tidal Zone* (Granta Books, 2017)

Rowling, J.K, *Harry Potter series* (Bloomsbury, 1997)

Pierce, Tamora, *Squire* (Random House, 2001)

Plath, Sylvia, *The Bell Jar* (Heinemann, 1963)

Tan, Shaun, *The Red Tree* (Simply Read, 2000)

Vonnegut, Kurt, *Mother Night* (Dial Press, 1961)

Woolf, Virginia, *The Waves* (Hogarth Press, 1931)

Non-fiction, essays, memoir

Angel, Katherine, *Daddy Issues* (Peninsula Press, 2019)

Campbell, Joseph, *The Hero With a Thousand Faces* (Pantheon Books, 1949)

Didion, Joan, *The White Album* (Simon & Schuster, 1979)

Drantell, Jennifer, *The Nomad Guide to the Tarot* (2014)

Fey, Tina, *Bossypants* (Reagan Arthur Books, 2011)

Gladwell, Malcolm, *Outliers* (Little Brown, 2018)

Heti, Sheila, *Motherhood* (Henry Holt, 2018)

Norwich, Julian of, *Revelations of Divine Love* (1670)

Pollack, Rachel, *Seventy Eight Degrees of Wisdom* (Thorsons, 1980)

Perry, Philippa, *How to Stay Sane* (Macmillan, 2012)

Snow, Cassandra, *Queering the Tarot* (Red Wheel, 2019)

Solnit, Rebecca, *A Field Guide to Getting Lost* (Penguin Books, 2005)

Solnit, Rebecca, *Storming the Gates of Paradise* (University of California Press, 2007)

Warner, Marina, *From The Beast to the Blonde* (Vintage, 2014)

White, E.B., 1973 letter as collected in *Letters of Note*, (Canongate, 2013)

Winterson, Jeanette, *Why Be Happy When You Could Be Normal* (Vintage, 2011)

Poetry, drama, and lyrics

Carter, Angela, 'William the Dreamer's Vision of Nature' from *Unicorn* (Profile Books, 2013) copyright © Angela Carter. Reproduced by permission of the Estate of Angela Carter c/o Rogers, Coleridge & White Ltd., 20 Powis Mews, London W11 1JN

Hall, Leslie, *Tight Pants / Body Rolls* (2010)

Jamie, Kathleen, 'The Hinds' from *The Bonniest Companie* (Picador, 2015)

Keats, John, 'On First Looking into Chapman's Homer' (1816)

Liu, Timothy, 'The Lovers' from *Don't Go Back to Sleep* (Saturnalia Books, 2014)

Oswald, Alice, 'Moon Hymn' from *Woods Etc.* (Faber & Faber, 2005)

Shakespeare, William, *As You Like It* (1623)

Shepherd, Nan, 'Strange Gifts of Pleasure' from *In the Cairngorms* (Galileo Publishers, 1934)

Classical works

Homer, *The Odyssey*

Plato, *Symposium*

Unknown, *Beowulf*

Articles and essays

Carson, Anne, translator, *Grief Lessons: Four Plays by Euripides* (New York Review of Books, 2006)

Gross, Terry, Interview with Maurice Sendak, *Fresh Air* (NPR, 1986)

Hall, Jerry, 'The Party Guide', *The Times* (2010)

Jung, Carl, *Visions: Notes of the seminar given in 1930-1934* (1934)

Marrin, Evie, *What The Fuck?*, (Interrobang, 2016)

Maslow, Abraham, A Theory of Human Motivation, *Psychological Review* (1943)

Nolan, Megan, 'The Pandemic Has Turned People into Tutting Scolds', *The Guardian* (2021)

O'Donoghue, Caroline, *Cheer Up Jen* (2015)

Pauley, Jane, Interview with Cher, *Dateline* (NBC 1996)

Sontag, Susan, 'The Double Standard of Ageing', *The Saturday Review* (1972)

Tierney, John, 'What is Nostalgia Good For?', *New York Times* (2013)

Wood, Denis, 'An Interview With Denis Wood' *The Believer* (2012)

Zimmerman, Jess, *Hunger Makes Me,* (Hazlitt, 2016)

Popular culture

Film and television

Anchorman: The Legend of Ron Burgundy (2004)

Casanova (2005)

Father Ted (1995-1998)

Frasier, Season 7, Episode 13: They're Playing Our Song (2000)

Karate Kid (1984)

The Lord of the Rings: Return of the King (2003)

The Matrix (1999)

Mean Girls (2004)

Moulin Rouge (2001)

Murder, She Wrote (1984-1996)

The Neverending Story (1984)

Star Wars (1977)

Working Girl (1989)

Games

The Legend of Zelda (series)

Street Fighter (1987)

Internet memes

Cats are a liquid

How it started, how it's going

Well, well, well, if it isn't the consequences of my own actions

Tarot decks

Further detail can be found in Chapter 13, but references have been made in the text to the following tarot decks:

Autonomic Tarot (Rough Trade Books, 2018)
Black Power Tarot
Carnival at the End of the World (2019)
Circo Tarot
Modern Witch Tarot (Liminal, 2019)
Numinous Tarot
Nomad Tarot
Rider Waite Smith (Rider Books, 1909)
Spolia Tarot (2018)
Tarot Sutra (Dorling Kindersley, 2000)
Transient Light
Wild Unknown (HarperOne, 2016)

Acknowledgements

So many thanks are owed to so many people.

Thank you to our personal Empress and Magician, Jo Unwin, who always suspected we were good for more than just light entertainment at Christmas parties, waited literally years for us to finally come to her with a book proposal, and then waved her magical agent wand to make it a reality.

Thank you to Bluebird, for publishing this book and giving us the space to share the stories of the tarot. Huge thanks to Hockley Spare and Carole Tonkinson for appreciating our long emails, longer video chats, and even longer spreadsheets. Thank you to the extraordinarily talented printmaker, Alexis Snell, and art director, Mel Four, for the book cover of our dreams. A second round of thanks to Mel for the beautiful illustrations that appear in each and every card section. Thank you to our copy editor, Chimene Suleyman and our authenticity reader, Cassandra Snow, for your careful readings and thoughtful advice on how to make this book better. And thank you to Jess Duffy and Sian Gardiner for helping us tell people about it!

Thank you to Treadwell's, and especially to Suzanne Corbie, for showing us the ropes, and also for putting up with our spirited and quite argumentative approach to learning the tarot almost every week for several months. Thank you to the wider tarot community, from whom we continue to learn and grow as readers.

Thank you to John Mitchinson for believing in us and Mathew Clayton for suggesting we take this show on the road. And thank you to Port Eliot Festival for getting the hag wagon rolling by giving us our first gig: reading two unsuspecting authors' tarot on stage. Thank you to Nina Stibbe and Lucy Mangan for being those unsuspecting authors (and we're sorry again, Nina, for revealing your secret wedding).

Thank you to everyone who's asked us to appear at their festivals, events, parties, wellness weeks, and launches over the years, and to everyone whose tarot we've read at them. Without you all, we'd never have written this book, because we'd probably never have realised that anyone would like to learn to use the cards the same way that we do. A particular thank you goes to Julian Mash, who's hosted some of our wildest and most sleep-deprived performances at End of the Road Festival for several years in a row. You're a brave man, Julian.

Thank you to everyone with whom and on whom we have honed our tarot skills and knowledge over the years, including friends, friends of friends, family members, colleagues, children, pets, writers, celebrities, and complete strangers in the pub. Special mentions go to Amy Winchester, Caroline O'Donoghue, Maddy Embleton, Caitlin Breeze, Reema Mitra, Steve Cownie, Becks Parnell, Anna Parke, Gavin Day, Alex Reichardt, Amelia Leeson, Grace Ang-Lygate, Melissa van der Klugt, Catriona Balfour, Phil Connor and Stephanie Theobald for your support and conversations, as well as the regularity and good grace with which you have agreed to be our querents.

Heartfelt thanks go to two sets of parents, Claire and Steve Wilson, and Jill and Graham Cownie, for being open minded and surprisingly supportive of this professional pivot. A little bonus thank you to Jill for emergency childcare (from Fiona) and for just being the most wonderful mum and sounding board for ideas for the book (from Jen).

Fiona would also particularly like to thank Max Lensvelt, who has been subjected to more of her tarot readings than anyone else. He believed in the book from the start and then had to deal with the consequences. Really, thank you (I love you). And to our son, our utter joy, in whose naps many sections were written: thank you, too, my love.

Jen would like to thank Gladstone's Library – the library you can sleep in! For her (as for many others) it's a magical, treasured place that allows her to live her best Hermit life, and was therefore instrumental in actually getting this book written.

Thank you to Timothy Liu for your generosity in allowing us to use *Don't Go Back to Sleep* as an epigraph, and to Robert Hyde at Galileo Publishing for permission to use a line from Nan Shepherd's poetry collection, *In the Cairngorms*.

Thank you to Leslie Hall, for penning the musical masterpiece *Tight Pants / Body Rolls*, as featured in the Eight of Wands. It just means so much to us.

And thank you to fate, fortune, the universe, the moon, blind chance, or whatever it was that put us in the same room as one another seventeen years ago so that we could become best friends, tarot readers and, eventually, authors. We're having an absolutely lovely time.

About the Authors

Jen Cownie and Fiona Lensvelt discovered a shared love of the tarot in their twenties, after taking a course together at Treadwell's, one of the UK's oldest occult bookshops. Drawn in by the beauty and richness of its visual symbolism, they quickly became immersed in the stories the tarot contains and the ways in which those stories can help people make sense of the full range of human experience – from the most significant moments in life to the smallest ones, and from the good to the bad to the completely baffling.

In 2018, they formed their stage show, Litwitchure, and have since appeared at events across the UK, introducing audiences to the tarot as a tool for self-exploration and conversation, and using the cards to interview artists and authors on stage. Their interviewees have included Pulp's Jarvis Cocker, Nina Stibbe, author of *Love, Nina*, Emma Jane Unsworth, author of *Adults* and *Animals*, and many more.

Fiona is also an editor at the publisher Unbound and was previously *The Times* Books commissioning editor, while Jen works as a strategy director for an advertising agency.

Connect with them online: @Litwitchure   litwitchure.com